Fabric
Manipulation

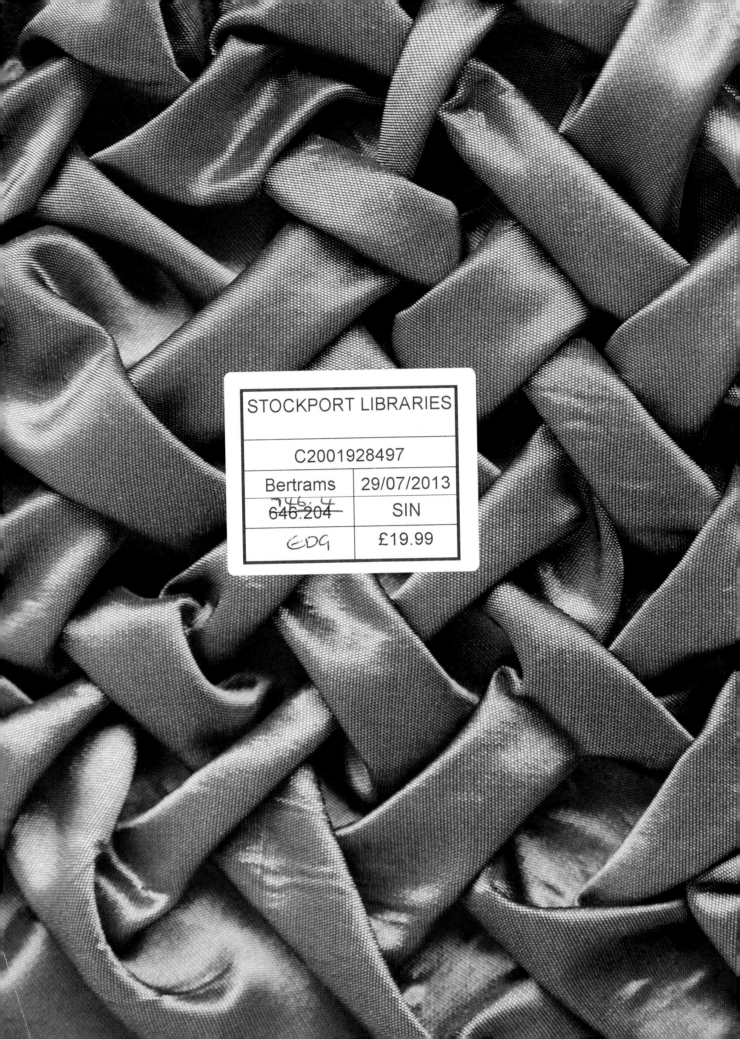

Fabric Manipulation

150 CREATIVE SEWING TECHNIQUES

Ruth Singer

David and Charles

www.stitchcraftcreate.co.uk

Contents

Pleat & Fold 22

Stitch & Gather

Introduction

Most of the techniques included in this book have come from my own study of historic clothing and vintage sewing books, or from my own experimentation. I was lucky enough to spend my 20s working in museums and getting the opportunity to indulge my love of historical costume. My fascination with decorative textiles has since become the basis of my career and I have never stopped loving looking at the amazing work of seamstresses from generations past, even if it now means pressing my nose up to the glass in costume museums rather than getting behind the scenes. Many of the best costume collections have produced books of close-ups of their historic clothing, or publish photos online so you can explore these kind of details yourself.

I also love to visit the best vintage clothes or antique shops to admire details in Victorian or couture dresses, and sometimes even to buy them. I have a small but growing collection of inspirational vintage and antique textiles and garments, which you can see on my website. Studying the details of clothes is where my design process starts.

Alongside the clothes themselves, I have amassed a huge collection of sewing books from the late 19th century to the present day, all of which have wonderful techniques and inspiration. It isn't just the expensive, older books that are the most exciting; most of my knowledge about English smocking has come from books published in the 1970s not the 1870s.

The final stage in my design process comes purely from experimentation, what I call 'playing with fabric'. I am a firm believer in design by making as fabric is mercurial; it has its own way of working and it doesn't always do what you want it to. Sometimes what appears at first to be a mistake turns out to be a new discovery or a route to something even better. I hope this book inspires you to create your own fabric manipulation experiments. The Design Guide gives you more tips on how to use the techniques and how to develop the ideas.

DESIGN GUIDE

Every time I teach fabric manipulation techniques someone creates a new variation. Almost all of the techniques will be transformed by using a different fabric or by tweaking the technique. Try the following tips to help you create your own work:

- Try radically different fabrics to those I suggest

- Combine fabrics in similar tones or try ombré (graduated shade) fabrics

- Use contrasting fabric textures – coarse and silky for example – on the same or similar techniques

- Use contrasting linings or backings

- Try techniques in transparent or opaque fabrics

- Play with the scale – thick fabrics often work better in large scale so try making giant versions

- Experiment with repetition – a technique can be transformed by using it en masse

- Print, dye, embellish or embroider the fabric before or after manipulation

- Think in 3D – explore how the techniques would work on objects as well as flat fabric

- Try the techniques in different materials such as neoprene, interfacing, paper or tyvek and combine with fabric

- With wearables, think about the weight and thickness of techniques and how the fabric will hang, as well as the practicality of wear and care

- Build techniques into clothing design by working the fabric manipulations before constructing the garment. Allow extra fabric for techniques such as smocking

- Customize clothing using techniques like pleated ribbon, Suffolk puffs and appliqué

- Create fabrics from scratch to make into one-off garments or accessories such as scarves

www.ruthsinger.com

Share what you make and interact with others

See more of my own work and the inspiration behind it

Explore additional content and videos

Browse a reviewed list of tutorials around the web on fabric manipulation techniques

Read features on other designers and makers who use fabric manipulation techniques

See couture and historic textiles examples

Fabrics and threads

In this section I have listed fabrics (and other materials) used to create the samples in the book, as well as many others that are of particular interest for fabric manipulation. For my samples, I have used fabrics that are mostly easy to use and visually clear, and generally I find natural fabrics preferable to synthetics.

Wool fabrics include thick wool felt, fine suiting or sateen and wool Melton often used for coats.

Fabrics: natural or synthetic?

My preference for natural materials is partly ecological, partly practical. Silk, wool and cotton behave in a more predictable way; they shape with heat and steam, they hold a crease, they iron flat most of the time. Synthetics are often harder to sew; they may be slippery and often don't hold a crease, which is why they are so popular for garment making.

There are some synthetics that work well with particular techniques and I have mentioned these below. Synthetics can often be 'set' by steam which is an exciting technique: try gathering or smocking a polyester fabric then steaming thoroughly; remove the stitching and the puckered shapes should hold. (Similar effects can be achieved with wool if stitched then felted.)

Your own experimentation will uncover many more variations on the techniques, using radically different fabrics, or substituting a synthetic fabric for my natural one. You will discover that many of the techniques will come out completely differently, worked on fine silk chiffon compared to thick wool tweed, for example.

There are hundreds of types of fabrics with specific names based on their yarn, construction or finishing technique. Some fabrics have different names in different parts of the world to add to the confusion.

Many fabric names (such as satin or velvet) refer to the production technique not the fibre, which can lead to confusion in fabric purchasing, where a synthetic (polyester satin) may be confused with a natural silk (satin).

Wool

For me, wool is the best fibre in the world. It can be as soft as cashmere or as coarse as carpet wool, with many grades in between.

Lightweight wools and light suit-weight wools: From vintage Viyella to fine wool Melton (a woven wool with a fine felted surface, which frays very little but hangs beautifully), there are some beautiful fabrics to work with, including English worsted or wool sateen fabrics. All of these will take a crease well and would be suitable for many Pleat & Fold techniques.

Wool crepe: This is a very fine fabric, particularly that made from merino sheep. It drapes well and is particularly suited to Stitch & Gather techniques.

Felt: Most commercial craft felt is actually made from acrylic or recycled polyester rather than wool. Better quality wool is now being produced with about 70 per cent wool combined with acrylic or viscose and it is this that I prefer to use. Wool Melton also acts like fine felt and can be felted even more by washing to produce a denser fabric if required.

Boiled wool: Sold by the metre/yard, this is usually knitted wool fabric, which has then been shrunk or felted. It can be used in the same way as felted jumpers.

Silk fabrics from top: dupion, habotai, chiffon, light dupion, silk/viscose velvet, taffeta, satin, crepe, and dupion.

Silk

Silk is probably the best fabric for use in most of the manipulations in this book, as it is so versatile and beautiful. Some of my favourite types of silk are listed below. Silk saris, vintage or new, can be a good source for fine quality silk fabric, but beware as many are actually synthetic.

Silk organza: This is a very finely spun silk woven into a gauze-like cloth, which is quite transparent. It holds a crease perfectly, it is very resistant to heat and its natural stiffness lends it to manipulations such as Box Pleating. Its transparency and limited fraying (particularly in the finer versions of the fabric) make it ideal for Shadow Work. Silk organza should not be confused with synthetic organza, which is a very different thing. Coarse organza makes a good pressing cloth.

Silk dupion/dupioni: Dupion silk is woven with fine silk in the warps and slubby silk in the weft to create a slightly lumpy, raw-looking fabric. It is popular for wedding and evening gowns because it is quite crisp and holds a shape, making it ideal for manipulations. Its crispness is partly due to fabric finishing treatments and these can be washed out to create a softer fabric that still has the crease-holding properties but less of the stiffness. As dupion frays very badly, it is not ideal for raw-edge applications, but works well bias-cut.

Satin: The term satin refers to a weave, which produces a diagonal or twill effect on the front face (similar to denim). Silk satin comes in a variety of weights with Duchesse being one of the heavier. A light silk satin is ideal for many of the gathered manipulations (see Stitch & Gather), while satin weave fabrics are ideal for techniques that rely on the play of light on the fabric's surface, such as Trapunto.

Silk crepe: This is another weave that is available in many different fibres, with polyester being the most common. Like wool crepe, silk crepe is a luxury fabric that has a beautiful drape and is ideal for gathered manipulations (see Stitch & Gather).

Silk velvet: Most commercially-available silk velvet is usually a combination of silk and viscose. Viscose is an engineered natural fibre that shares many characteristics with linen and silk, particularly in terms of drape. Silk/viscose velvet is a fine fabric that works well for Stitch & Gather techniques.

Chiffon: Available in silk or synthetic versions. Silk chiffon is expensive and troublesome to use in garments, but works well in manipulations where its transparency and light weight can be put to good use.

Habotai: This usually refers to a lightweight opaque silk, commonly used for linings or for silk painting. Habotai is one of the less expensive types of silk and it is a staple in my fabric stash. It takes a crease, is not too slippery, and works well in gathering techniques (see Stitch & Gather).

Taffeta: Silk taffeta is a crisp, stiff fabric, much copied in synthetics although originally made in silk. Silk taffeta is often 'shot', which means the warp and weft threads are different colours, making the fabric look different depending on how the light hits it (in the 19th century this was known as 'changeable'). Synthetic taffeta is a good alternative to silk taffeta in many situations, and I like to use vintage rayon taffeta from the 1940s and 1950s for crisp, pleated manipulations or for smocking.

Silk ribbon: Pure silk ribbon is hard to buy (I often have to buy vintage if I want one more than a few centimetres wide) but it gathers and drapes much more effectively than synthetic ribbon.

Plant-based fabrics

The main plant fabrics are cotton and linen although bamboo, hemp, ramie and other bast fibres are becoming more common, and viscose is just one of a range of engineered natural fibres.

Linen: This comes in a range of weights, from lightweight to very heavy. It has a natural stiffness to it, which can easily be enhanced with starch. It takes creases well for Pleat & Fold techniques, and when pre-washed it softens up making it ideal for Stitch & Gather techniques. Linen frays considerably, even when cut on the bias, which makes it ideal for a fluffy Stitch and Slash technique.

Handkerchief linen: This is very fine, lightweight linen that works well for smocking and pleating, although it is at risk of crushing making it difficult to use in American Smocking or any technique with a 3D effect.

Cotton: Like linen, cotton comes in a range of weights. Plain weave, medium-weight shirting cotton or light quilting cotton is my favourite type of cotton, and best of all is organic cottons, which will have no finishing or stiffening treatments added. Fabrics such as these take a crease effortlessly but also drape and gather well. Many finely spun and woven cottons will not fray excessively, and one of the finest cottons readily available is cotton lawn, made popular by Liberty, but also widely available in plain colours.

Cotton organdie: This is generally a fairly coarse weave using stiff threads, and the fabric is also stiffened after weaving. It is very crisp making it good for structured pleats and 3D shaping.

Cotton sateen: This is a twill weave (see Satin), which has a soft sheen and a smooth surface. It is a great all-round fabric in place of silk satin.

Bamboo: This is available in a range of weaves and knits. It can be extremely soft and is good for Stitch & Gather manipulations.

Calico and muslin: These cheap fabrics are great for experimentation. Calico is generally quite stiff although it will soften with washing and handling. It is ideal for Pleat & Fold techniques as well as Stitch & Gather techniques once softened. Muslin is loose-weave cotton that drapes well, making it effective for Stitch & Gather techniques. Finer quality versions of muslin are also available, such as voile.

Hemp: This is a good alternative to linen and it is available in a range of weights; hemp-silk mixes are beautiful fabrics.

Cotton jersey: Knitted fabrics for clothing are made in a range of fibres including polycotton, wool, viscose and synthetics to the less-common silk. Jersey is a great fabric to use for hand-stitched Stitch & Gather manipulations, but machine sewing can be more difficult as the fabric can stretch.

Cotton velvet: This has a shorter pile than silk velvet, but it should not be confused with thick, synthetic-mix upholstery velvet, which is very hard to manipulate. Cotton velvet drapes well and is ideally suited to many Stitch & Gather techniques, as long as you work with large pieces and keep stitches large to create big gathers – it will bunch up unattractively if you try to use small stitches.

A selection of plant fibres including linen, lawn, flannel, velvet, muslin, bamboo, organic cotton and organdie.

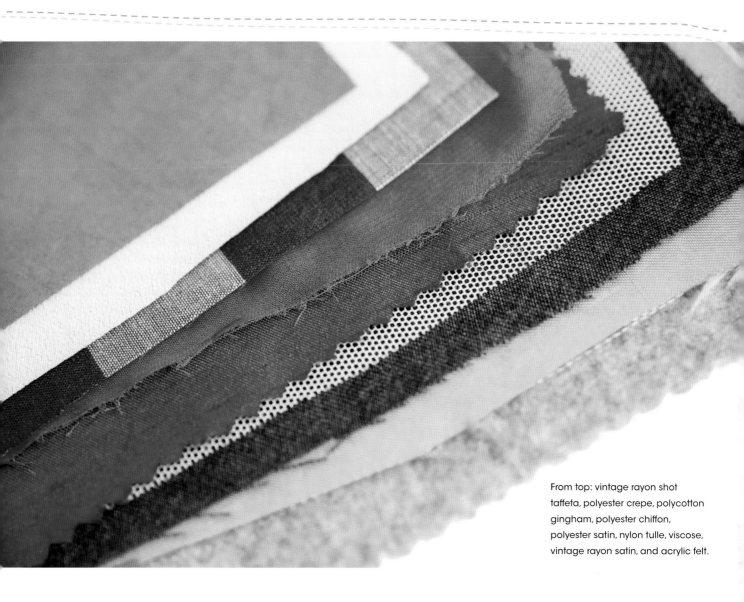

From top: vintage rayon shot taffeta, polyester crepe, polycotton gingham, polyester chiffon, polyester satin, nylon tulle, viscose, vintage rayon satin, and acrylic felt.

Other fabrics

Fleece: Polyester fleece is an interesting fabric to experiment with. Compared to what is available in the shops, buying old garments yields a greater variety of thicknesses and qualities.

Net and tulle: Cheap netting is usually nylon and its inherent stiffness can be useful in many applications. Tulle usually refers to a finer version that is less stiff and more drapey, although still usually synthetic. Silk tulle is the finest of all, but it can be expensive and difficult to buy; it can be found more cheaply in the form of damaged vintage wedding veils.

Leather and suede: Fake animal skins look very much like leather but do not behave in the same way, and often have the problem of synthetic slipperiness. The finest suedes and leathers can be manipulated with great success, particularly for gathering and smocking techniques (see

Sttich & Gather). If ethics or price are a concern, look for old suede skirts, which can yield a large amount of good fabric.

Polycotton: This is generally the cheapest and most readily available fabric around. While is it hopeless for anything requiring a crisp finish and a fold, it is great for Stitch & Gather techniques. As with all fabrics, there are different qualities; a heavier, more expensive polycotton made with good cotton will be best to work with.

Rayon: I like to use vintage fabrics and find that vintage rayon is a good place to start. It comes in matt crepe, satin and taffeta weaves and generally holds a crease well (as a consequence it can be hard to iron). The satin version is good for Stitch & Gather techniques.

Threads

Sewing threads

I prefer to use good quality pure cotton general sewing thread as I like the thickness and the matt surface of the thread. Cheap threads should be avoided as they will be poor quality and liable to snap and snarl up in the sewing machine. In addition, there are a few other threads that will come in useful.

Polyester thread: This is vital when the stitching is under a lot of strain such as tightly pulled gathering. Polyester thread is generally finer than cotton and has more sheen. It should always be used with real leather and for anything with stretch. Avoid poor-quality cheap threads.

Silk threads: Available for hand and machine sewing, these are ideal for use when the stitching shows on a silk fabric as it should disappear into the surface.

Quilting thread: Specially spun threads for machine and hand quilting have a high twist and are less likely to fray and tangle. They are excellent for any hand sewing where you are working with very long lengths of thread.

Embroidery threads

Both natural and synthetic embroidery threads are available, with natural threads being more matt and synthetics more shiny, on the whole. Silk and rayon are the most common fibres used for embroidery threads after cotton, although you can also buy wool as either a fine crewel thread or chunky tapestry wool. Two popular types of embroidery threads are:

Stranded cotton (floss): This is made of six threads loosely twisted together, and you can separate the strands and use as many threads as you like.

Cotton perle: This is a twisted thread not suitable for separating. It is less likely to go fluffy than stranded cotton (floss), so it is ideal for Direct and English Smocking where the thread is visible.

A selection of the sewing threads I used regularly.

Stuffing and wadding (batting)

Techniques such as Trapunto require a stuffing material. The choice of stuffing depends on the finished use of the project. Where an item will need to be laundered, a polyester toy stuffing is the best to use. For the finest details wool stuffing, ideally merino, which is very fine and readily available for needle felting, is better. Other natural and engineered stuffings are available too, such as lyocell and cotton wadding.

Quilt wadding is available in a huge range of fibres and different weights. The cheapest is polyester and thinner cotton wadding is becoming more common. Wool, silk, bamboo and recycled polyester are just some of the newer waddings that are now available. Some waddings also have heat-activated glue on the surface for ease of layering quilts together.

Ribbon

Most commercially-available ribbon is made from polyester although some rayon and blends are available. Satin ribbon that is shiny on one side only is the best for pleating techniques, while double-side (double-faced) satin is hard to get to hold a crease. Pure silk ribbon is great for pleating although wide ribbon is hard to source. For more details on sourcing, see Suppliers. Vintage ribbon often provides a good alternative. I use a lot of vintage rayon grosgrain for pleating techniques as it is often quite stiff, holding a crease well, and it is quite easy to buy. Modern cotton or synthetic grosgrain is also good, but you may struggle to get it to hold a crease. Every ribbon is different so experimentation is vital. Gathering techniques require a soft, draping ribbon, which can be hard to source. Vintage rayon or taffeta ribbon is good, as are the top quality modern ribbons from specialist suppliers.

Vintage ricrac, ribbon and
haberdashery from my collection.

Tool guide

Most of the techniques in this book require nothing more than a sewing needle, thread, scissors, an iron and some marking chalk. However there are some tools that I use regularly and recommend for particular techniques in this book. Always use the best quality tools and equipment you can afford. Changing from basic tools to professional tools makes the world of difference in the ease and success of your sewing.

Hand sewing

Always use the finest needle possible: ideally it should be about the same thickness as the thread you are using. While it is tempting to use larger needles as they have large eyes and are easy to thread, there are several good reasons not to: large needles can be hard to push through dense-weave fabrics; an over-large needle will leave unnecessarily large holes in the fabric and may even damage the fibres. If the needle doesn't glide effortlessly through the fabric then it is too big. The more expensive brands are worth buying if you hand sew a lot with fine fabrics, and mid-range price needles are good for general sewing, but avoid cheap multi-packs completely if you are serious about sewing.

Sharps: These are the best needles to use for general hand sewing in sizes 5-10 (I generally use size 8 which is very small but works much better than a larger needle).
Appliqué: These short, fine, sharp needles are also very useful for many of the techniques included in this book.
Milliners or sashiko: These needles are longer and can be useful for gathering stitches.
Tapestry: These are blunt needles with a large eye and they are designed for canvaswork embroidery.
Crewel: These are smaller than tapestry needles but have a larger eye than sharps; they have a sharp point and they are useful for thicker threads.
Leather: These needles have a chisel-like triangular tip that glides through leather easily. They are available for hand or machine sewing.

Other useful equipment

Thimble: This is essential if you do a lot of hand sewing. It goes on the middle finger of the sewing hand to help you push the needle through the fabric. (A finger protector is useful for the other hand if you find you prick your finger.) Modern thimbles are more flexible and easier to use than traditional metal thimbles, and you can even get stick-on metal or plastic thimbles just for the fingertip.
Needle grabbers: These small rubber discs allow you to grab and pull on a needle. Small pieces of old rubber gloves or fine suede can also work.
Tweezers: These are really useful for stuffing trapunto, pulling out stubborn thread ends from ripped seams, and for removing fluff and threads from the bobbin case.

Machine sewing

Most of the techniques listed in this book can be achieved using any basic sewing machine, but if you are planning on upgrading your machine, there are a few features I would recommend for professional results.

Moveable needle: This feature allows you to move the needle left or right from the centre, enabling closer stitching on piping or zips. Higher-spec machines have a wider range of movement options.
Presser foot pressure: This feature allows you to vary the pressure on the presser foot – lighter for heavy or thick fabrics and heavier for fine fabrics. It makes the sewing of these fabrics much easier.
Fix stitch: This feature automatically reduces the stitch length to about 0.5mm for a couple of stitches, which fastens off the thread neatly without the need to reverse. (You can also do this manually.)
Knee lift: This is a knee-operated lever that raises the presser foot, enabling you to keep both hands on the sewing.
Presser foot height: Machines that have more clearance under the presser foot will make it easier for you to work with thick pieces of fabric.
Working space: Machines designed for quilters have more space between the presser foot and the main body of the machine, giving you more space to work, whatever type of sewing you are doing.
Quilting table: An extension table that attaches to the free-arm of the machine and this allows much more room for you to work and helps to keep larger pieces spread out flat.

Machine feet

Even-feed foot: This may also be referred to as a walking foot or dual-feed foot. It may not be cheap but it is worth the investment. A bulky-looking foot, it has an extra set of feed dogs (teeth) that move the top

Even-feed foot.

fabric at the same speed as the underside fabric to stops layers sliding around and separating. This is particularly useful when working with quilt layers, velvet, slippery fabrics, or two different fabrics together.

Quilting guide: A metal bar that attaches to the presser foot to gauge the distance between rows of straight stitching.

Clear view foot: This is a plastic alternative to the basic metal zigzag foot but the clear plastic and markings make it much easier to use. I keep this foot on my machine all the time.

Clear-view foot.

Darning foot: This is essential for free-motion sewing and embroidery.

Ruffler foot: This attachment creates automatic pleats in a wide range of sizes. More information can be found in Pleat & Fold: Knife Pleats.

Ruffler foot.

Gathering foot: For quick and easy gathering, this enables you to make gathers on the underneath fabric and sew it directly to flat fabric on top in one step.

Gathering foot.

Note: When choosing a machine needles, you should use the finest needles for fine fabrics and thicker ones for denim and upholstery fabrics, just like hand needles.

Pinning

Sometimes you will need to keep the fabric manipulation in place as you work so choosing the right pin for the job can be important. As I often pin fabric to the ironing board when I am working, I find glass-headed pins are essential as plastic ones would melt on contact with the iron. Here are a list of the pins I use most often.

Long glass-headed pins: These are easy to pick up, easy to use, and they will not melt under the iron.

Sequin pins: These tiny pins can also be useful. As they are very short and have flat metal heads, they can be pushed right into the ironing board as I work.

Extra-long flower head quilter's pins: These are perfect for working through several layers of fabric and as they are extra fine they will not damage fabrics.

Appliqué pins: Short, sharp pins with small plastic or glass heads, these are very useful for small pieces and fine work.

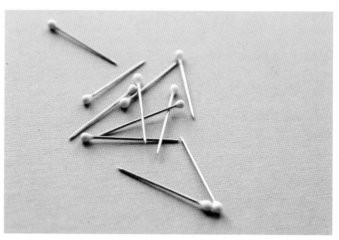

Appliqué pins.

Sewing clips: These small plastic clips are designed to hold together layers of fabric without the need for pins. They are incredibly useful when working with fiddly layers, or with fabrics that might be damaged with pins, or when a third hand is required. I recommend them particularly for many of the techniques in the Pleat & Fold section.

Sewing clips.

Gluing

Glues can also be used sometimes to hold layers together and there is a range of glues suitable for fabric.

High-tack fast-acting PVA: This is the best for fiddly work that needs fastening rapidly.

Water-soluble fabric glue: This can also be used for temporarily holding pieces together before embroidery, quilting or appliqué. It is available in liquid form, glue stick and as a spray, which is useful for large quilts. It does not damage the sewing machine but you should not iron the glued fabric as this can either set the glue permanently or make it harden. The long-term stability of this type of glue is not good – it may yellow or harden with age – so it will need to be washed out.

Quilters' masking tape This is a narrow, low-tack tape, which can be applied to the surface of the fabric to mark straight lines. The glue should leave no residue or mark on the fabric but always test before use, and do not leave the tape on for a long time or iron over it.

Cutting

There are a few essential tools required for cutting fabrics and it really does pay to buy the best quality you can afford – don't be tempted to buy cheap multi-pack scissors.

Shears: Large scissors designed for sewing are made with a bent handle so the blades will run along the table as you cut fabric. If you look after them well, they will last for years, if not decades. I like sprung shears, which are kinder to the hand when cutting lots of fabric.

Embroidery scissors: Extra-fine tipped, super sharp scissors are vital for snipping threads, for trimming reverse appliqué, for unpicking stitches and for many delicate tasks. I replace mine every year to ensure that they are really sharp.

Medium-sized scissors: A sharp pair is useful for cutting small pieces of fabric such as appliqué shapes.

Pinking shears: These are useful for decorative edging and for finishing fabrics to reduce fraying.

Rotary cutter These are ideal for cutting large amounts of fabrics with straight lines. Always use together with a self-healing cutting mat and a safety ruler: never use just an ordinary plastic ruler as you will shave the edge off the ruler and you will risk cutting yourself. Replacement blades are required regularly and can be expensive. Pinked blades are also available to cut decorative edges.

Slashing tool: A tool designed for cutting numerous layers of fabric with ease and useful for the Stitch and Slash technique.

Marking

Marking fabric is vital for many of the techniques in this book. There are many different methods that you can use, depending on the fabric being worked, the detail required and the final use of the piece. There are also several methods for transferring designs from paper to fabric.

Tools for marking

Traditional tailor's chalk: This is most commonly available in blocks or wedges, but you will find these to be of limited use, as a finer point is usually required for the techniques in this book. While it is possible to sharpen chalk with a craft knife, chalk in pencil form and powdered chalk in refillable pens is better, and those designed for quilters will be most useful: most are water-soluble, which is fine if you are planning to wash the finished piece but may not be suitable in all situations. Where the markings are made on the reverse of the fabric, pencil will be fine, and even ordinary graphite pencil can be used, but not on light fabrics/ threads as the graphite will show through or smear on the thread. Some quilting pencils come with an eraser, which is useful, and these work best on smooth cotton fabrics.

Air-erasable and water-soluble pens: For detailed marking, these types of marker tool are best. While both are good, air-erasable is better where markings are needed on the front of the fabric. Always test first though to check that the markings do actually vanish sufficiently. Water-soluble marks can be removed by light spraying with water, but this can mark some fabrics with water spots, so testing is essential. Never iron over markings as they may set.

Soap slivers: Useful for marking fluffy fabrics such as wool felt.

Resin marker: Useful for marking straight cutting lines and fold lines.

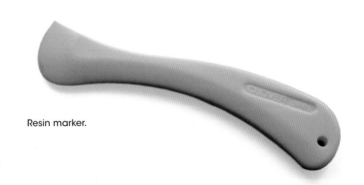

Resin marker.

Transfer methods

Heat-transfer pencils: These useful pencils are designed for embroidery and they leave a water-soluble mark. Use the pencil to draw over the paper design (on the same paper or onto tracing or baking paper), turn the paper over and press the design onto the fabric, being careful not to move it around.

Dressmakers' carbon paper: This paper comes in a range of sizes and colours and can also be used to trace a design. Place the carbon paper colour-side down on the fabric, place the design on top and trace over the lines using pencil or a tracing wheel. Waxed paper (freezer paper) can be used in the same way on dark fabrics. Always check that the marks made are suitable and that they don't damage your fabric.

Tracing: You can often trace directly onto the fabric by taping both design and fabric to a window (in good daylight) or to a light box. You can make your own large light box with a sheet of opaque acrylic propped up at each corner and a table lamp underneath.

Ready-made printed transfers: Embroidery patterns and smocking dots can be bought that are printed with heat-transfer inks and ready to use. Simply place face down on the fabric and press following the manufacturer's instructions.

Measuring

A good-quality tape measure is essential and you may also find the following useful:

Rulers: I use a range of rulers ranging in size from 15cm to 60cm (6in to 2ft) as well as metal metre (yard) sticks for larger projects: I find that 45cm (18in) and 60cm (2ft) are particularly useful sizes but these are hard to find.

Quilters' rulers: These plastic gridded rulers have rough spots on the underside to stop them moving around on top of the fabric. They are very useful when used in combination with a rotary cutter but they are also handy for general measuring and marking. The most commonly available quilters' rulers are American brands that have imperial measurements, although it is sometimes possible to get European or

A quilter's ruler has angles marked on it making it ideal for cutting bias-cut fabric strips.

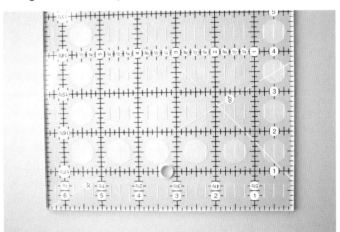

Japanese rulers in metric. They come in a wide range of sizes and also in different template shapes for patchwork.

Templates: I have a large collection of plastic and metal patchwork and appliqué templates, particularly circle shapes, which I use regularly.

French curves: These dressmakers' tools can be very handy for creating curved designs.

Sewing gauge: This little gadget is one of my favourite tools. Unlike a normal ruler, the measurements start from the very end, which enables accurate measuring, and the sliding marker makes it easy to check repeated measurements quickly and accurately.

Sewing gauge.

Pressing

Careful pressing of your work is vital for good results. Iron the fabric before you cut out and always press when the instructions say so.

Iron: A good iron is essential for good sewing. If possible, keep an iron specifically for sewing. A steam-generating iron with a separate tank is the best and it should ideally have a Teflon sole plate. A mini iron or a travel iron is useful when working with small, fiddly pieces.

Pressing cloths: These are vital when working with delicate or special fabrics and they will avoid damage to either the iron or the fabric. Teflon pressing cloths are great for fusible webbing or interfacing and will protect your iron from any excess glue: for best value buy oven sheets in kitchen shops rather than sewing shops. For general pressing, however, I prefer to use silk organza: it is remarkably resilient to high heat but allows steam through to the fabric, and its transparency means you can see what you are doing. Buy a metre (yard) of good quality organza and rip the edges rather than cutting to stop it fraying too much; avoid hems as these will leave marks on the fabric when pressing.

Pressing bars: These heatproof plastic strips are designed for pressing narrow widths of bias tape. They can also be used for pressing and folding straight edges. You can also use strips of cardboard however, which you will be able to write on, cut and mark.

Stitching techniques

Good basic sewing skills are vital for success when working fabric manipulation techniques, but you don't need to be an expert. The stitches and tips below are all you need to make any of the techniques that is featured in this book. Remember that good tools are vital as well, so use the best needles and thread you can get.

Useful hand stitches

Careful, neat hand sewing will make all the difference to your fabric manipulation techniques looking great and staying intact. Remember to fasten the thread at the start and end of the stitching too.

Backstitch

Backstitch is used to make firm and permanent seams. It can be used in place of machine sewing.

Slip (invisible) stitch

Slip stitch is a quick and easy hand stitch used to join two pieces together, particularly for appliqué. The thread shows on the back but hardly on the front.

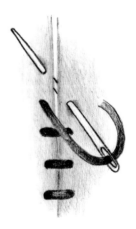

Fishbone stitch

This stitch can be used to pull two edges together without creating a ridge, and it is particularly useful for Trapunto. Fasten or knot the thread then, beginning underneath one edge, bring the needle out about 3mm (⅛in) from the raw edge and then into the gap. Go through the gap and back out 3mm (⅛in) from the edge on the opposite side and continue.

Blanket stitch

This is a useful decorative method of finishing an edge or attaching an appliqué.

Bring the needle out of the fabric, make a loop and hold it with your left thumb. Put the needle in the fabric diagonally opposite where the thread came out, and back out again vertically.

Pull up the stitch and continue.

Machine stitching techniques

Many of the techniques in this book use hand sewing but for some a machine is preferable. A basic machine will be fine for most techniques although you may want to buy some accessories (see Tool Guide).

Pivoting

This method is used to change direction in machine sewing. It is also used to turn sharp corners when making cushions for example, and to make minute adjustments to the sewing direction when sewing a Scalloped Edge or other detailed shapes. Sew as normal to reach the pivot point. Turn the flywheel so the needle is down in the fabric, lift the presser foot and manipulate the fabric as required. Lower the presser foot and continue sewing as before.

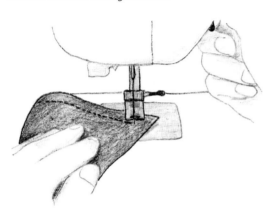

Fastening

Where the stitching does not show and when bulk is not a problem, you can finish off the sewing by reversing (backstitching) a few stitches. To fasten the thread without reversing, reduce the stitch length to 0.5mm (or the smallest stitch length possible) and make two or three stitches (some machines have an automatic setting for this). Alternatively, leave the threads long and pull the top thread through to the back by pulling on the bobbin thread; knot the threads together.

Free-motion sewing

Free-motion sewing enables you to 'draw' on fabric using the machine. The design is created freehand, although you can draw the design onto the fabric first. You can move the fabric from side to side as well as forwards and backwards. When working with single-layers of fabric, you may find a stabilizer fabric placed behind it helps to avoid puckering and stretching: tear-away stabilizer is designed for machine embroidery; if you are using a fine washable fabric, try a wash-away stabilizer that will disappear completely.

The easiest way to learn free-motion embroidery is by working with the fabric in a hoop. You hold onto the hoop and move it – and the fabric – around under the needle. Without a hoop it can be hard to move the fabric sufficiently, unless it is very firm.

First drop the feed dogs on the machine. Check the sewing machine manual to find out how to do this: most new machines have a switch, but some older machines may have a metal plate that you fit over the feed dogs.

Use an embroidery or darning foot. Use machine embroidery thread in the needle – a co-ordinating sewing thread will be fine in the bobbin. You may need to remove the presser foot to fit the embroidery hoop under the needle; replace the presser foot after.

Set the stitch length and width to 0. Moving the fabric under the needle creates the stitches: the further you move it, the bigger the stitches will be. Some machines will have a speed setting: slow will result in larger stitches, whilst faster running gives smaller stitches.

Put the presser foot down. Start with the machine running slowly and move the hoop around to create lines and swirls, or follow a drawn design if you prefer. You will be able to speed up as you get more practice.

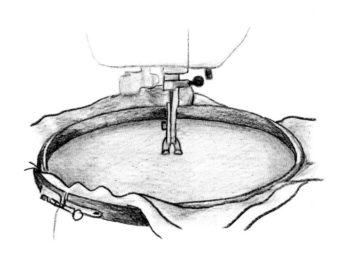

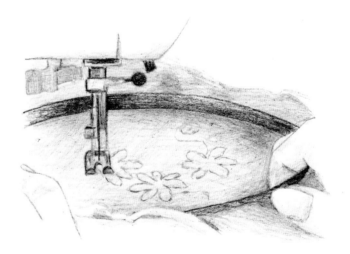

Other techniques

This section covers a few of the techniques that are useful for many of the manipulations in this book including how to use freezer paper to create templates, how to cut on the bias and other specialist methods of working with fabrics.

Bias cutting

Woven fabrics are made with vertical warp threads and horizontal weft threads, which run from selvedge edge to selvedge edge. The lines of these threads are known as the straight grain. The true bias runs at a 45-degree angle to the straight grain. Woven fabric is considerably stretchier on the bias and easily pulls out of shape. Fabric cut on the true bias will fray considerably less than straight grain cut and some fabrics will not fray at all on the bias. Bias-cut fabrics will also take a curve, sew into curved shapes and mould to fit curves using steam pressing.

To cut bias strips from straight grain fabric, fold the fabric so the warp and weft threads line up and you have a neat diagonal fold. Press the fold and unfold. Mark the width of strips required using the fold line as one edge. Once cut, be careful not to stretch the bias out too much by supporting the fabric. You can purposely stretch the bias out (particularly in floppy fabrics like chiffon) by pulling the strip along its length and ironing it out.

Freezer paper templates

Freezer or waxed paper can be used to make templates that are ironed onto the fabric temporarily. Iron-on templates can be used to cut out precise shapes, as templates for fluffy fabrics such as felt which cannot be easily drawn on, and to press over for Appliqué. There are three different methods.

Fold over templates

This technique is used for creating templates for Appliqué where you fold over the raw edges to the back.

Cut a piece of freezer paper slightly larger than the motif and draw the motif on the paper side; cut out. Place the freezer paper wax-side down onto the reverse of the fabric. Press with a warm iron until the paper has stuck. Cut the fabric out around the motif allowing for a 5mm–1cm (¼in–⅜in) seam allowance. Leave the template in place and press the edges over. Tack (baste) the seam allowances in place if required.

Raw edge motif

This technique works well for cutting very precise shapes out of particularly thick or fluffy fabrics such as wool felt. Use fine, sharp embroidery scissors to cut out.

Cut a piece of freezer paper slightly larger than the motif and draw on the paper side. Cut the motif out. Place the freezer paper wax-side down onto the reverse of the fabric. Press with a warm iron until it has stuck. Cut around the motif without a seam allowance, following the outline closely. Remove the paper only when you are ready to apply the motif – leaving it on prevents the motif from stretching or fraying before use.

Cut through paper

Cutting through both paper and fabric works best on lighter fabrics as it is hard to get a precise edge when working on thick felt.

Cut a piece of freezer paper slightly larger than the motif and draw on the paper side. DO NOT cut the motif out. Place the freezer paper wax-side down onto the reverse of the fabric. Press with a warm iron until the paper has stuck. Cut around the drawn line, through both paper and fabric. Remove the paper when you are ready to apply the motif.

Clipping and notching curves

Curved seams must be shaped to make them lie flat when ironed. Inward curves should be clipped so the fabric can spread out. Outward curves need to have little V-shaped notches cut into them. Use small, sharp scissors to cut into the seam allowance: do not cut too close to the stitching or the seam may tear.

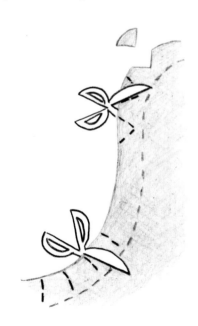

Using interfacing

Interfacing is a type of fabrics used to stabilize, strengthen and support fabrics, and sometimes to stiffen. There are many types of interfacing but for the samples in this book I have used iron-on woven or non-woven only. These are interchangeable but non-woven is cheaper and more readily available.

Iron-on interfacing has heat-setting glue on one side that enables it to be pressed to the reverse of the fabric. Iron-on interfacing will stop the fabric fraying, stretching and creasing. Lightweight interfacing should be used in most cases (heavier weight interfacing can make fabrics very stiff and hard to sew). Experiment with different types and weights to create the effects you wish to achieve.

To apply interfacing, always cut to shape before ironing on. Place the fabric wrong side up with the interfacing glue (rough) side down on top, ensuring the interfacing does not overlap the edges of the fabric to avoid transferring glue to your ironing board. Cover the whole piece with an organza or cotton pressing cloth (do not press without a pressing cloth as non-woven interfacing is synthetic and can melt). Follow the instructions on the interfacing and press with light steam and medium heat. Do not move the iron around as this can cause the interfacing to wrinkle.

Stiffening fabrics

Spray and wash-in fabric stiffeners including starch and fabric glue can be used to make fabrics hold a crease or behave differently. All fabrics will react differently so experimentation is vital. Spray starch can be very useful in pleating and folding soft fabrics and also for making appliqué motifs, but the effect is only temporary until washed.

Felting

Wool felt can be made from old jumpers and knitwear to create a dense, non-fraying, material for manipulation. The combination of hot water, agitation and soap makes the wool fibres fluff up, grab each other and matt together, creating a thicker, fluffier version of the original fabric. Different knits will come out at different thicknesses and some don't felt at all. Machine washable woollens are not suitable for felting so look for 'HAND WASH ONLY' labels. While a small amount of non-animal fibre is fine, the main components should be wool, lambswool, cashmere, angora or alpaca.

Wash the knitted fabrics on a medium to hot wash (some knits will only felt at 90°C while others can work at 40°C). The felting will be improved if you have a full load, but be aware that felting knits may shed fluff over the rest of your wash, so it is best to felt separately from a general wash. It is best to place the pieces in an old pillowcase tied with string. Beware also that dyes may run from the knitwear, so either wash similar colours together or put in a dye-catching cloth.

Once the wash has finished, hang up the pieces straight away as the spin cycle can leave creases in the wool that are hard to remove. There is no need to tumble dry felted wool. If it hasn't felted as much as you want, put it through another wash. When dry, press with a very hot iron and lots of steam to get any remaining creases out.

Pleat & Fold

Knife pleats

Knife pleats are usually seen as creases in pleated skirts, and they appear in all kinds of traditional clothing worldwide. Pleats are usually stitched down at the top and allowed to open out at the bottom to create shape and movement in garments.

MATERIAL AND DESIGN NOTES

- Knife pleats are usually made using straight pressed creases and this technique works best with natural fibres.

- They can be made very precisely by careful measuring, or by eye to create a softer, more organic look.

- For the basic method described, each knife pleat is 2.5cm (1in). The fabric will be reduced to one third of the original width.

Basic method

The basic method describes making evenly spaced pleats, each one butting up to the next.

1 Fold the fabric over the end of the ruler and fold back again at the marked point which is the half-width measurement or 2.5cm (1in) in this sample. Pin the pleat in place at top and bottom.

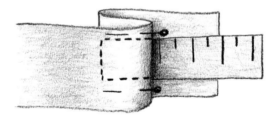

2 Remove the ruler and place the 2.5cm (1in) mark on the underside fold. You cannot see this fold so lift the fabric carefully to check the placement. Reposition the ruler and fold the fabric back again to the 2.5cm (1in) mark. Pin as before, then repeat as required.

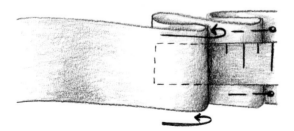

3 If you are enclosing the pleats in another sewn seam, tack (baste) across the top of the pleats to hold them together temporarily, otherwise machine sew across all folds to keep the pleats in place.

The basic method describes making pleats 2.5cm (1in) wide.

The basic method can be applied to make knife pleats of any width, such as these narrow pleats which are approx 1cm (⅜in) wide.

Variations on the basic method

Vertical stay stitching

The knife pleats are made following the Basic Method, and then stitched down vertically to hold them in place. The stitching is usually the same length as the width of the pleat, which is 2.5cm (1in) in the sample shown, but regularity is not essential.

Knife pleats with vertical stay stitching.

Horizontal stay stitching

In this sample, narrow knife pleats have been stitched at the top and also lower down to contain the pleats before they spread out.

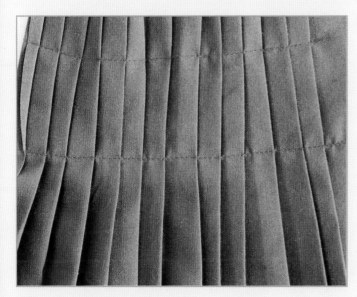

Knife pleats with horizontal stay stitching.

Bias edge

A triangle cut on the bias can be knife pleated in the same way as the Basic Method to reveal the reverse of the fabric. This is very effective for double-sided fabric, such as the woven wool used in the sample shown.

Bias edge knife pleats.

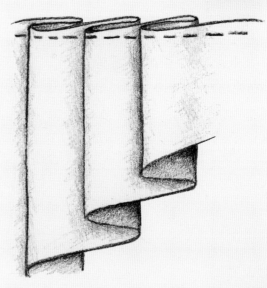

Edged pleats

For this variation, the top side of the pleats is edged with ribbon before the fabric is folded. The pleats are made the same width as the ribbon and the space between ribbons is exactly two ribbon widths.

1 Mark the pleat and ribbon placement on the fabric allowing for two ribbon-widths in between. To give you the pleat fold line, mark the centre point between ribbons. When placing the ribbons, make sure each is completely straight following the grain of the fabric.

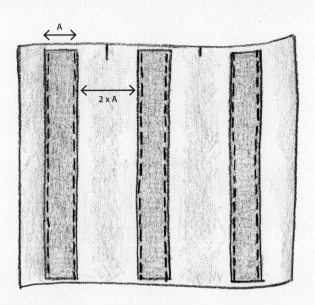

2 Make the pleats as for the Basic Method, placing the end of the ruler on the mark in the middle of the gap.

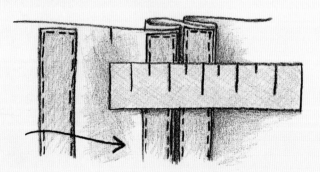

3 Fold the fabric over so the right-hand edge of the ribbon meets the pleat width on the ruler.

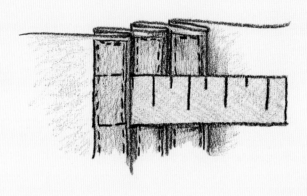

Edged pleats create striking effects in movement and would look stunning on a skirt.

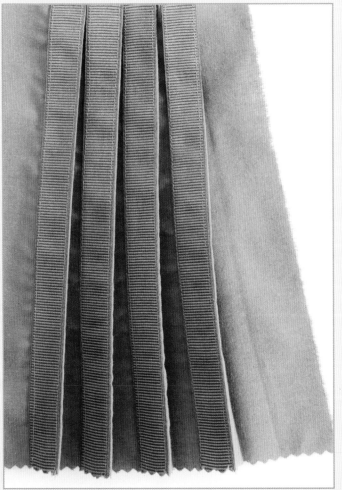

Inset pleats

Knife pleats, or any other kind of gathered, ruffled or pleated edge, can be set into another piece of fabric as an inset ruffle or an inset square.

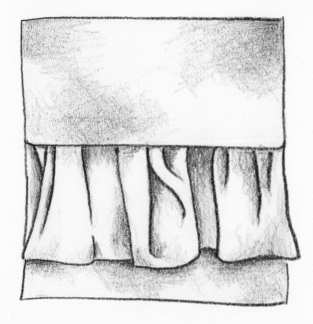

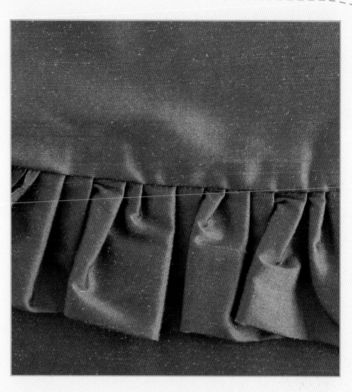

For an inset ruffle: The fabric is folded double then pleated along the top edge. The ruffle is then applied between two pieces of fabric following In-Seam Trims: Basic Method (see Apply & Layer).

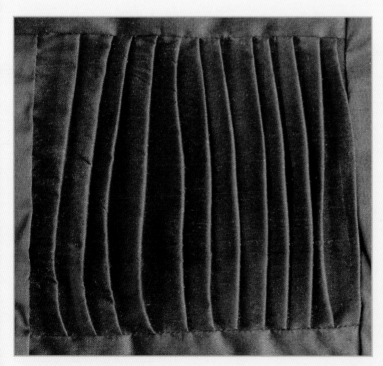

For an inset square: The pleating can be made on just one edge of the fabric or on both upper and lower edges. In the sample shown, the pleats have been made in the same direction on both upper and lower edges, and stitched in place; the stay stitching has been enclosed and hidden when setting the pleated piece into a log cabin square (see Apply & Layer: Stuffed Squares).

Machine pleated

Pleating directly on the machine produces pleats much faster than the precise measuring, pinning and stitching described in the Basic Method. The resulting pleats are irregular and often slightly wonky, but they will become more regular with practise.

Begin sewing a little way along the upper edge of the piece to be pleated. Stop sewing with the needle down and take a pinch of fabric just in front of the presser foot. Fold the pleat under so it just sits by the presser foot. Hold in place by hand and continue sewing.

Machine ruffler foot attachment

A ruffler foot attachment can be very useful for creating gathers and narrow pleats and it is a lot simpler to use than you might expect. This works in a similar way to the Machine Pleated technique, but instead of you having to hand-manipulate the fabric into pleats before it goes under the presser foot, the ruffler foot attachment does this for you. It has a little shovel-like plate, which shunts the fabric under the foot creating a small pleat. The ruffler foot attachment has settings for making the pleats on every stitch or further apart as you prefer (see samples). Pressing the fabric after pleating makes the effect more like tiny pleats rather than gathers.

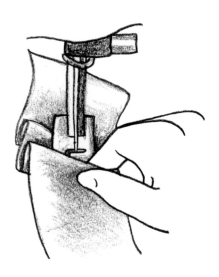

Machine ruffler foot attachment.

Machine pleating direct to base fabric

In this sample, the ribbon is pleated in the same way as described for Machine Pleated fabric but the ribbon is sewn directly onto the base fabric. Draw a line on the base fabric as a guide to the ribbon placement. Begin sewing, manipulating the ribbon pleats as you go and ensuring the base fabric does not get puckered.

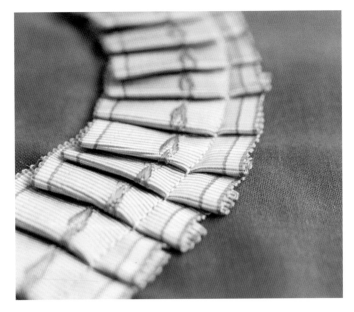

Ribbon pleated directly onto base fabric.

Ruffler foot attachment set to make pleats on every stitch to create close gathers or pleats.

Ruffler foot attachment set to make pleats on every
6th stitch on bias grain.

Ruffler foot attachment set to make pleats on every
6th stitch on straight grain.

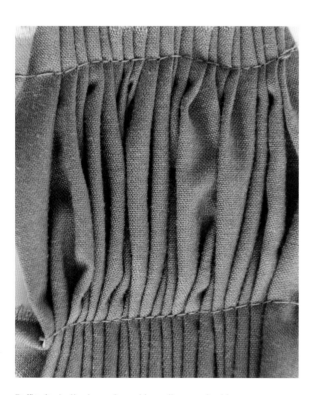

Ruffler foot attachment used to gather or pleat top
and bottom edges.

Ruffler foot attachment set to make pleats on every 12th stitch
on bias grain.

Box pleating

Box pleats are flat, usually deep, pleats, often found in jackets and tailored clothes. They were very popular in the luxurious, draped gowns of the 18th century. Box pleats, described in the Basic Method, have the pleat on the back, while inverted box pleats have the pleat on the front.

MATERIAL AND DESIGN NOTES

- The pleat is made in two halves: each side of the pleat is half of the total required pleat width.

- When measuring the pleat, use a ruler with a sliding marker/sewing gauge.

- Make sure the fabric is cut on the straight grain – making pleats on off-grain fabric is more difficult as it will not crease neatly.

Basic method

1 Working from the front of the fabric, mark the centre point of the pleat. Place the ruler so the required width is at the centre point.

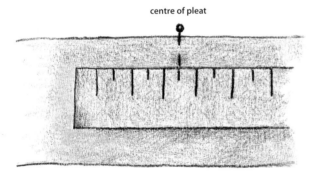

centre of pleat

2 Fold the fabric over the ruler and fold it back again at the marked centre point. Pin in place, making sure the crease is straight and that it follows the straight grain of the fabric. Press if required.

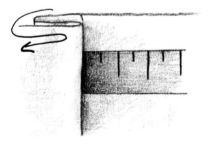

3 Flipping the ruler over, repeat step 2 to make the other side of the pleat.

4 Sew the completed box pleat down following one of the two methods illustrated in the sample.

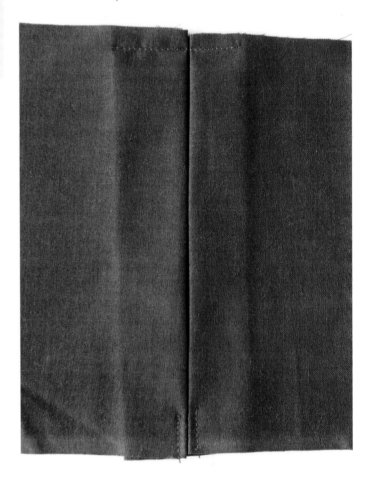

The box pleat can be secured in one of two ways. The top of the sample shows stitching straight across simply to hold the pleats in place. The bottom of the sample shows stitching along the inner folds to create a neater, more refined finish; this keeps the pleats flatter and is often used on garments, although the pleat would be stitched at the top only to allow the pleats to open out.

Box pleat variations

Manipulated box pleat

This is made in the same way as the Basic Method, and stitched with straight stitching top and bottom. The folded edges of the pleat are then folded back and either pressed or stitched in place to create a decorative finish.

The manipulated box pleat could be made in a contrasting colour by adding a strip of fabric into the main fabric before making the pleat. The strip should be the width of the finished pleat plus seam allowances.

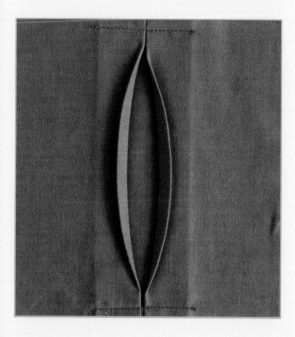

Manipulated box pleat.

Inverted box pleat

An inverted box pleat is made in exactly the same way as the box pleat described in the Basic Method, but this time working from the back of the fabric.

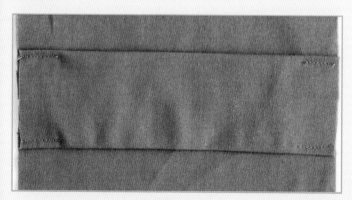

Inverted box pleat: in this sample the stay stitching is made on the outer edges of the pleat on the front of the fabric.

Double and triple box pleats

Add extra pleats to the box pleat by repeating step 1 of the Basic Method, once for a double box pleat, as shown in the sample, and twice for a triple box pleat.

Double box pleating works well with medium-weight fabrics. You could also combine it with the ribbon-edged pleat technique (see Knife Pleats).

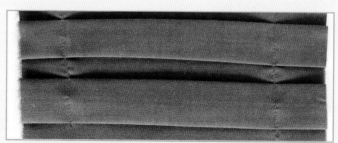

Narrow inverted box pleats can be placed close together. In this sample they have a half-pleat width between them.

Decorative box pleating

This decorative trim technique has been used for centuries on clothing and furnishings and was very popular in the 18th century. Often seen worked on ribbon, it can also be made with prepared bias-cut strips (see Other Techniques) or a fabric tube pressed flat. There are many folding variations to the Basic Method, several of which are included on the following pages.

MATERIAL AND DESIGN NOTES

- Use fabric that takes a crease well and which is not too soft, such as cotton lawn or silk dupion.

- Allow for a length of ribbon, fabric strip or tube a little more than three times the length of the finished pleats; for example, for 30cm (12in) of pleating, use a 100cm (39¼in) length – this allows for a few centimetres (couple of inches) at each end of the pleating.

- The pleats made must be exactly the same width as the ribbon or fabric strip used. The example given is based on a 6cm (2⅜in) wide fabric strip, so the half-pleats will be exactly 3cm (1³⁄₁₆in) deep.

- For the folding techniques to work correctly, the pleating must be precise. The pleats should be close together and completely square.

Basic method

1 First make a pleat measure from a piece of lightweight card – in this case approx 5cm (2in) wide by 15cm (6in) long – and mark a line HALF the width of the fabric strip from one end, which is 3cm (1³⁄₁₆in) in this sample. This marked line will be your guide when making the pleats.

2 Start with the fabric strip the right side up and mark 6cm (2⅜in) – or the width of your fabric strip – along from the end with a pin. Place the card measure so the drawn line is on the pin. Fold the fabric strip over the measure (folding to the left) so the new fold meets the marked line. Hold in place and remove the measure. Pin vertically to hold the pleat. This is the first half of the first box pleat.

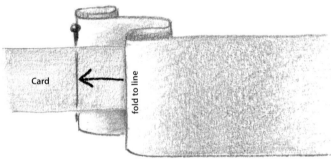

Box pleating on vintage rayon grosgrain ribbon.

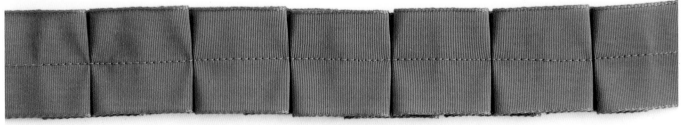

Box pleat on ribbon.

3 Turn the fabric strip over to the wrong side. Hold the measure so that the marked line is on the fold. Fold the strip over the measure again so the folds meet. Remove the measure and pin the pleat.

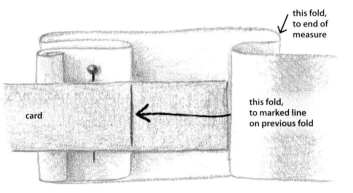

this fold,
to end of
measure

this fold,
to marked line
on previous fold

card

4 Turn over and repeat with the marked line on the fold and continue, turning the fabric strip over each time, until you have enough whole pleats or run out of fabric. The folding direction should follow the diagram below.

5 Press the pleated strips flat. Use chalk or vanishing pen to mark a line down the centre of each strip and machine sew along the marked line to secure the pleats in place. Alternatively, use the marked line to sew the pleated strips directly onto a backing fabric, such as a cushion cover or an item of clothing.

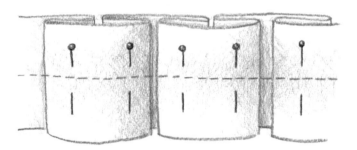

By using transparent silk organza strips rather than ribbon, the box pleat becomes ethereal and light. The strips are cut on the bias which allows the pleats to curve beautifully whilst not fraying.

Folding variations for basic box pleat

Once the box pleats have been made, the pleats can be pressed or left unpressed then manipulated, folded or stitched into many different designs.

Pinch top

The tops of each pleat are stitched together. Lift the top layer of the top and bottom edge of the pleat and bring together at A. Use tiny stitches to secure the two sides at the mid-point.

Pinch top.

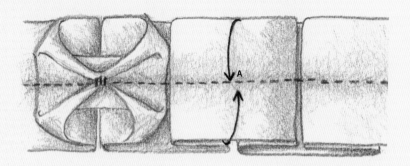

Point to point

Fold the opposing corners of the pleat over to the centre line and press to keep them in place. You can stitch the folded pleats into position if you wish: fasten the thread on the reverse side and bring the needle up from the back, make a couple of stitches then fasten on the back.

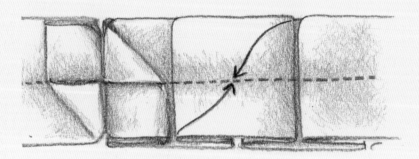

Point to point.

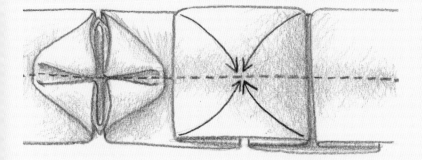

Squares

These are made in a similar way to Point to Point, but this time each corner of the pleat is folded to the centre and stitched down.

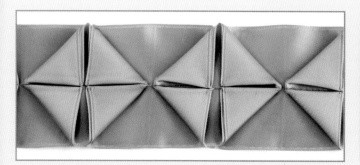

Squares, pressed.

Squares, unpressed.

Diamonds

Take the centre bottom edge of the pleat, top layer only, and lift it up so point A meets point B, holding the bottom of the pleat in place. Press the folds flat so that what was the bottom edge of the pleat becomes the vertical 'mouth' of the diamond.

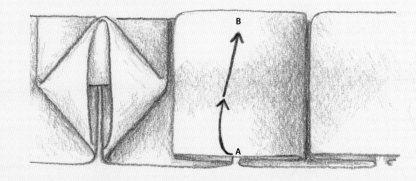

Squashed diamonds

Work in the same way as the Diamonds variation, but this time take the centre bottom edge of the pleat, top layer only, and lift it only half way up from the centre line, then press flat so the bottom points meet.

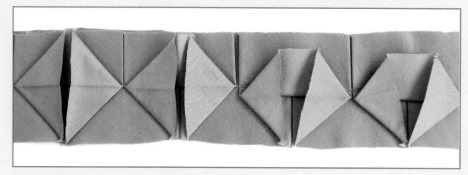

Diamonds (left) and squashed diamonds (right).

Sawtooth diamonds

Lift the top edge of the pleat and fold over to the bottom edge. As you do so, allow the underside folds at either side to fold back into triangles so that points A and B are in the correct place as shown on the diagram. Repeat.

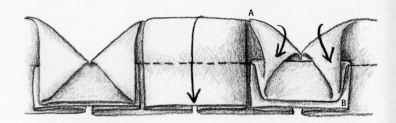

Sawtooth diamonds.

Arrows

Lift and fold the top edge of the pleat to the bottom edge. Allow the underside folds on the left-hand side to fold back to make a triangle, but on the right-hand side, press the underside folds flat to form a triangle pointing in the same direction.

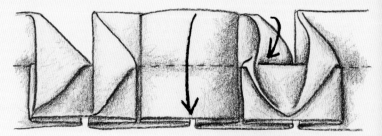

Arrows.

Up and down triangles

Make the first fold as for Sawtooth Diamonds, lifting the top edge to the bottom edge and allowing the underside folds to make opposite triangles. Then fold the top layer only of each corner to the centre – points A and C to point B. Press flat and hand sew in place if required.

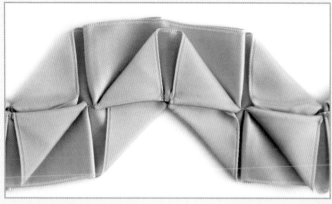

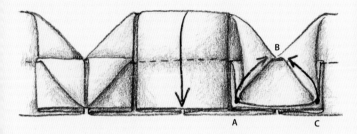

Up and down triangles: you can make all the folds in the same direction, or alternate top and bottom as shown.

Tuck under triangles

Make Up and Down Triangles, then fold points A and C underneath towards point B. Press and hand stitch if required.

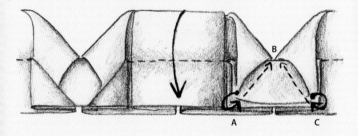

Tuck under triangles.

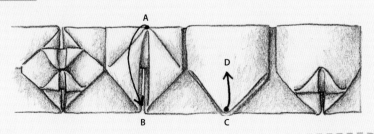

Diamond fold back.

Diamond fold back

Make Diamonds and press flat. Lift the top of the diamond and fold down from point A to point B leaving the underside folds in place. Press flat, then fold back partially so point C comes to the centre at point D.

Turn the work through 180 degrees and work the same technique on the lower half to complete the fold. Stitch at the centre if required. To keep the folds soft, do not press during construction; use finger pressing only, and then stitch the final fold.

Points to centre

Lift the top edge of the pleat and fold so point A meets point B (slightly off centre) and the lower folded edge lies along the stitching. Repeat to fold the bottom edge of the pleat.

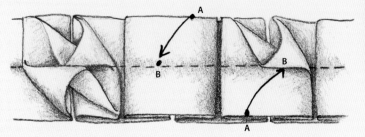

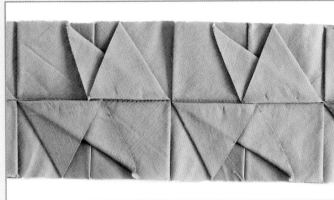

Points to centre.

Points to centre offset

On the top edge, lift the top layer of the pleat so point A comes to point B (in the centre of the pleat) and press the folds flat to form a triangle. On the lower edge, bring point C to point B, making sure the raw edge is vertical. Press the triangle flat.

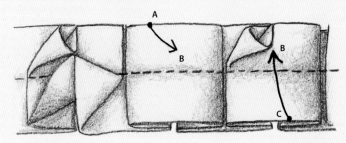

Points to centre offset.

Points to centre overlap

On the top edge of the pleat, lift the left corner A and fold down to point B, allowing the underside pleat to fold back. Press flat. Repeat on the lower edge, bringing C to D, once again allowing the underside pleat to fold back. You can choose to overlap the top fold over the bottom fold, or vice versa as preferred. Press flat.

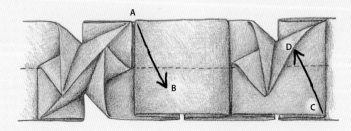

Points to centre overlap.

Half star

Working on the left side of the pleat, fold the top edge to make an arrow fold (see Arrows); press. Then, holding the triangle flat (where the arrow points), fold the pleat back over from point A to B so the folded back triangle is hidden under the top part of the pleat. Fold from point C to D, revealing your first fold. Press and sew in place if required. Repeat on opposite corners.

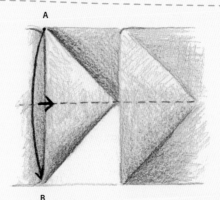

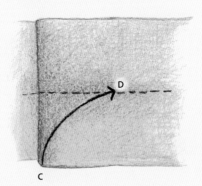

Half star.

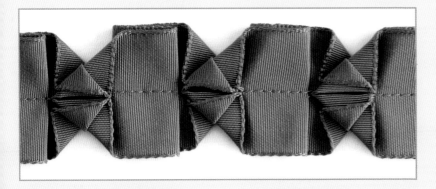

Half star spaced

Repeat the Half Star fold on both the top and bottom edge of the left side of the box pleat. Leave the other half of the box pleat unfolded. Move on to the next box pleat and repeat, folding the left side only.

Half star spaced.

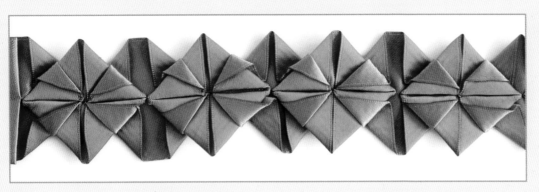

Star

Make the Half Star fold on all four corners of each box pleat.

Star.

Decorative box pleat variations

Spacing out the pleats and combining different techniques on the same piece can be very effective. Experimenting with different pleat widths, spacing and folding techniques can create new, exciting effects.

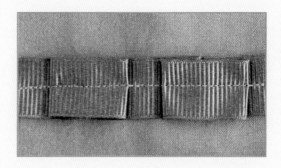

Box pleat spaced apart: here, the pleating is folded and pinned, then the whole piece is stitched directly to the base fabric.

Box pleat spaced apart
Following the Basic Method, make a box pleat but leave regular gaps between each pleat: in this sample a gap half the width of the pleat was left.

Double and triple box pleats
Follow the Basic Method but repeat the folding on steps 2 and 3, twice for double pleats and three times for triple pleats.

Double box pleats

Triple box pleat.

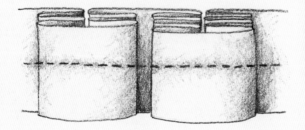

Side-stitched triple box pleats
Make a triple box pleat then fold the top two layers together vertically, and stitch just at the sides.

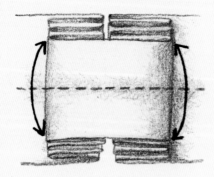

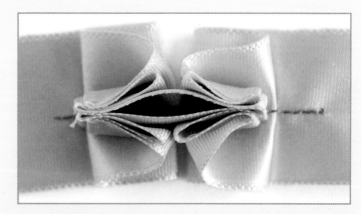

Side-stitched triple box pleat.

Knife pleat and box pleat combination

Knife pleats can also be stitched along the centre and folded as box pleats to create more variations. This technique works well on straight grain strips or extra wide ribbon.

Basic centre-stitched knife pleat

This version of knife pleating is made in even measurements, half the width of the piece of ribbon or fabric being pleated. This, combined with centre stitching, makes it work in much the same way as box pleating as far as folding variations are concerned. It is effectively half a box pleat repeated in the same direction.

Use a card measure or a ruler to get the correct size of pleat. In the sample shown, the fabric width used was 7cm (2¾in), so each knife pleat is 3.5cm (1⅜in), that is half the width of the fabric used. The fabric will be reduced to one third of the original length.

1 Fold the fabric back over the end of the ruler to fold at the marked point, which is 3.5cm (1⅜in). Pin the pleat in place top and bottom.

2 Remove the ruler and place the half-width measurement where the underside fold is. You cannot see this fold so lift the fabric carefully to check the placement. Fold the fabric back again to the 3.5cm (1⅜in) mark. Pin as before, then repeat as required.

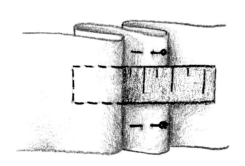

3 Machine sew along the centre of the pleats. Press if required.

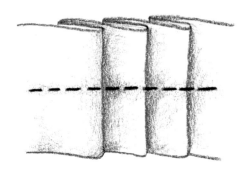

Basic knife pleats made on crisp organic cotton.

Exploring folding variations

Many of the manipulations so far described can also be worked on knife pleats and knife and box pleat combinations. One basic sample is shown but many are possible.

Triangle or chevron folds: Working on the top edge, fold the corner of the pleat to the centre, bringing point A to point B; continue to create single triangles or repeat on the lower edge for chevrons.

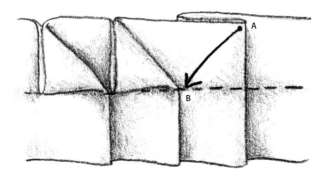
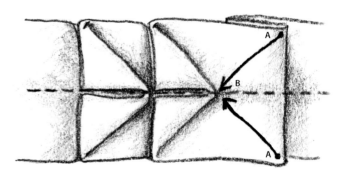

Triangle (left) and chevron (right) folds.

Knife and box pleats can be combined to create new folding variations. In this sample there are three left-facing knife pleats and two right-facing knife pleats, creating a box pleat off-centre. Each pleat is folded in the chevron method with the box pleat creating the Pressed Squares variation.

Project Idea:
Box Pleat Neckpiece

I created this piece whilst experimenting with the possibilities of box pleating using stiff silk organza. It is a dramatic, show-stopping piece. This example is quite large, but a smaller version would be more wearable: keep the length the same but use a narrower strip, and make smaller box pleats.

Technique: Box Pleat Pinch Top
Material: Silk organza

• Using bias-cut strips of silk organza about 6cm (2⅜in) wide, make the basic box pleat all along the length (see Basic Method).

• When the pleats are complete, DO NOT PRESS. Adjust to the correct length to fit over your head and join into a circle.

• Pinch the top of each box together following Pinch Top and hold with a tiny stitch or spot of fabric glue. Repeat on the reverse side with the opposite boxes.

Spaced and irregular box pleats

Tall, narrow box pleats are folded and manipulated in different ways to the regular square pleats as they cannot be folded to the centre to create square variations.

Rectangular box pleats point to centre

In this sample, the pleats are made half the height of the fabric to create tall, rectangular pleats from a straight-cut tube of cotton fabric.

Prepare as for Basic Method and stitch along the centre. Take the top edge of the box pleat and fold to the stitched line, A to B, allowing the edges to fold out into a diamond shape.

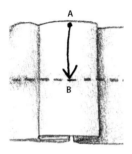

For the twisted variation, take the centre of the bottom pleat at point A and fold to point B. Press flat. Repeat for the top pleat in the opposite or the same direction.

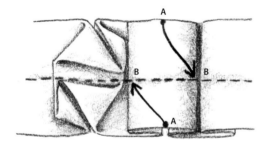

Adding a twist to the folds creates a kite-shape that can point in either direction. Try making them in sets of four with the points to centre for a star-effect.

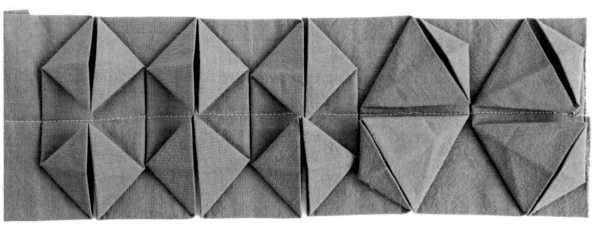

Rectangular box pleats point to centre (left) and twisted variation (right).

Rectangular box pleats triangle fold

In this sample, the pleats are 5cm (2in) high but only 3.5cm (1⅜in) wide, creating unsymmetrical folds. The folds on the left side are made using the Points to Centre fold (see Folding Variations for Basic Box Pleat) and those on the right, use the same method but in the same direction top and bottom, not reversed.

Rectangular box pleats triangle fold made on bias-cut silk.

Rectangular spaced pinch top box pleats

In this sample, the pleats are spaced at regular intervals, and the spaces between pleats are the same width as the pleats. The sample is made using a tube of bias-cut fabric and this creates soft folds best left unpressed. Bring the bottom and top edges together and sew by hand as in Folding Variations for Basic Box Pleat: Pinch Top.

Rectangular spaced pinch top box pleats made in a tube of bias-cut silk..

Dips and diamonds

This sample is based on a 19th century skirt trimming made of crisp violet silk. The tall box pleats are made in the usual way, but the pleats are just half the width of the fabric. The distance between each pleat is the same as the height of the fabric.

1 Cut a length of fabric 24cm (9½in) wide and approx 1m (1yd) long. (To create a longer piece, join pieces together.) Fold in half with right sides together and sew into a tube; press and turn out. Alternatively, simply fold and leave the bottom edges raw as in this sample.

2 Starting at the right side and 6cm (2⅜in) in from the raw edge, make the first half-pleat 3cm (1¾in) wide. Make the other half of the pleat, then continue spacing the pleats 12cm (4¾in) apart, using the diagram for guidance on how to measure. Continue to the end of the fabric length, then sew along the centre. Remove all pins and press flat.

3 Make the small folds first. Take the top edge of the box pleat and fold to the stitched line, A to B, allowing the edges to fold out into a diamond shape Next make the deeper folds. Lift the top edge at point A and bring to point B allowing the underside folds to open back out. The underside folds should not break on the stitching line but approx 1.5cm (⅝in) above the stitching line. Press flat.

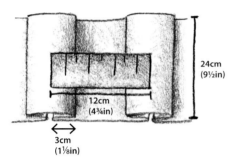

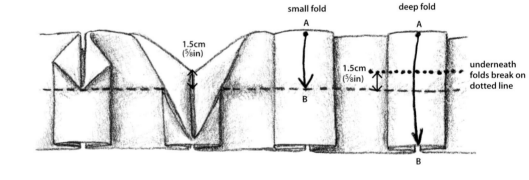

Dips and diamonds made in a wide strip of straight-cut silk folded in half lengthways with fold shown here at top.

Lined tuck box pleat

This sample is made using tucks folded flat to create box pleats. The effect is much the same as Rectangular Box Pleats Points to Centre but as the box pleats are made with tucks, no stitching is visible on the front. *Note:* The lining technique can be used with any of the construction methods and is not specific to this technique.

To create a lined fabric, cut two pieces of fabric on the straight grain the finished height plus 2cm (¾in) and three times the length plus extra for ends if required. Sew the two pieces of fabric right sides together along the long edges, using a 1cm (⅜in) seam allowance. Press the seams flat, then press open, and turn the piece through to the right side. Press the edges again, trying to keep the lining and front fabric even.

Create evenly-spaced tucks following the directions in Tucks. The spaces should be the same width as the tucks, as shown in the diagram. Press the tucks open and flatten out so that they butt up to each other in the same way as Basic Method box pleats.

Now fold over the top edge of each tuck towards the centre allowingn the edges to fold out into a diamond shape. Repeat along the bottom edge.

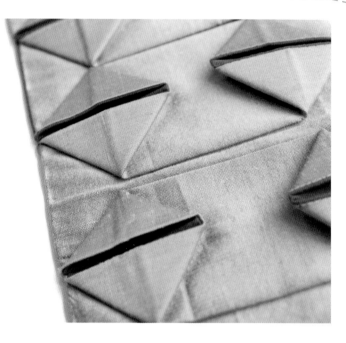

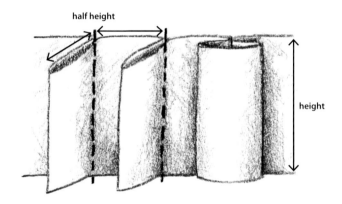

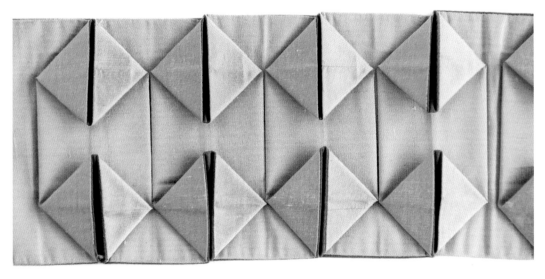

Lined tuck box pleat: silver silk lined with purple cotton for contrast. Both fabrics should be similar weight and not too thick.

Tucks

Tucks are similar to pleats, but they are sewn all along their length to stick up from the fabric. They can vary in size from tiny pin tucks to large flaps of fabric, which can be manipulated in a number of ways. The fabric will reduce by two-thirds for tucks made right next to each other, less if you space the tucks out as described in the Basic Method.

MATERIAL AND DESIGN NOTES

- Sewing lots of tucks can be problematic: the fabric slips and the tucks go out of alignment as you sew, resulting in a wonky set of tucks.

- Synthetic fabrics are much harder to manipulate into neat tucks, whilst crisp cotton is the easiest to work with.

- Your chosen fabric should have a clear grain and take a crease well. To start, make sure the fabric is cut precisely square to give you very straight edges to work with. Striped fabric is good to practise with, as you can fold and sew along the stripes, but make sure the stripes are an even width, not varied.

Basic method

1 Working on the right side of the fabric along the top edge make marks every 2cm (¾in), leaving 3cm (1⅛in) or more at each edge.

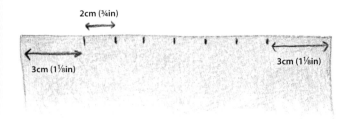

Basic spaced tucks, unpressed.

Basic spaced tucks, pressed.

2 Again working with the right side of the fabric facing up, fold over the right edge so the first two marks match, poking a pin through to check they line up. Make sure the fold is straight along its whole length. Check the fold is on the straight grain and the top and bottom edge line up. Finger press, then pin in place with pin heads pointing to the right.

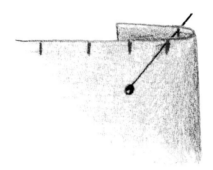

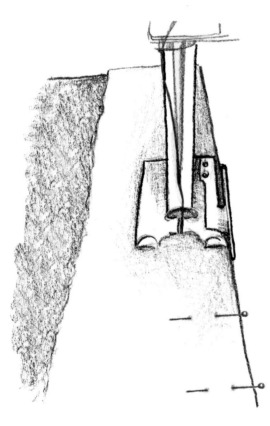

3 Place on the machine with the fold to the right and the excess fabric to the left. Sew the tuck ensuring you keep the seam allowance the same all along the fold. When making small tucks like this, you can use an edge guide foot to keep the distance even, or use the guidelines on your sewing machine. If your machine does not have guidelines, place a piece of masking tape on the machine bed the correct distance from the needle. Keep the edge of the fold on the line as you sew, making sure you do not allow the underside layer of fabric to twist.

4 Make the next fold with the first fold you made tucked underneath and the excess fabric to the right. Sew the second fold in the same way as the first making sure you don't catch the earlier tucks when you sew. *Note:* You may find it easier to sew the tucks from the bottom edge to the top, so the tucks already made are on the top, so it is easier not to catch them when sewing subsequent tucks.

Tuck variations

Once the basic tuck technique has been mastered, you can experiment with variations, particularly Tuck and Fold which has many possibilities. Twin needle tucks are also included in this section.

Close tucks

These tucks are made in the same way as the Basic Method but with smaller spaces between each tuck, for example 2cm (¾in) wide tucks would have 1cm (⅜in) gaps between each tuck; this makes the folded edge of each tuck butt up to the stitching of the previous one. Sew with the previously made tucks facing up and keep the left edge of the machine foot following the previous stitching. .

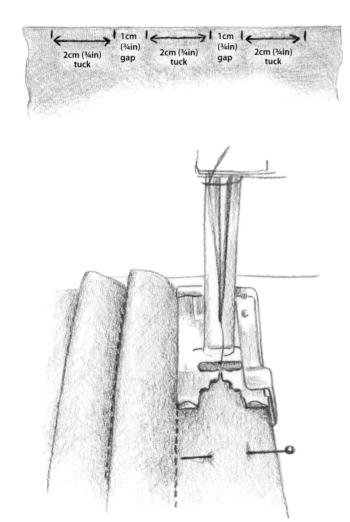

Close tucks, unpressed.

Pin tucks

Narrow pin tucks are made in the same way as the Basic Method with each tuck just a few millimetres wide, and spaced widely or closely together as you choose. In this sample, the tucks have a total width of 8mm (⁵⁄₁₆in) with 8mm (⁵⁄₁₆in) in between tucks. Narrow tucks can be sewn with the fold following the edge of the machine foot, or by using a ¼in patchwork foot for a very narrow tuck.

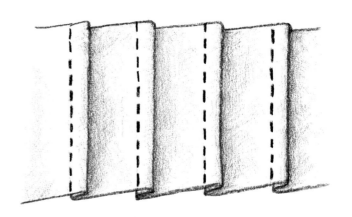

Pin tucks: these tucks are sewn down for 6cm (2⅜in) then released. For a neat finish, reduce the stitch length to 0.5mm rather than reverse stitching.

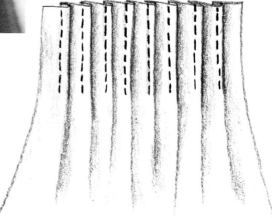

Twin needle pin tucks

For a quick version of very narrow pin tucking, use a twin needle. The effect is created by the stitching on the back pulling the fabric into a small pucker along the stitching line. The degree of puckering can be altered by changing the machine tension. This technique works best on crisp fabrics where the effect is obvious, and the sample is made in silk dupion. The tucks don't show up well on thick fabrics, and very soft fabric needs careful testing and tension adjustments or it will pucker too much. A matching thread shows the texture best; contrasting thread distracts from the texture. Although technically a tucking technique, this is very similar to corded quilting (see Apply & Layer: Corded Trapunto).

1 Insert the twin needle into the machine. Add a second thread to the machine's additional spool holder. Thread the machine with both threads together and thread each needle separately. Test sew and adjust the tension to create the desired effect.

2 Mark the lines on the front of the fabric. Sew at a gentle speed, manipulating the fabric so the stitching follows the marked lines.

3 Reduce the stitch length to 0.5mm to finish, rather than reversing.

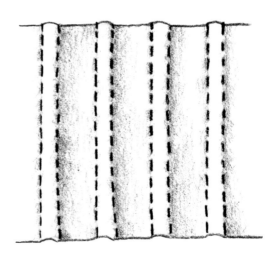

Twin needle pin tucks: sewing straight rows on straight grain fabric, front of fabric.

Twin needle pin tucks: following curved lines, front of fabric.

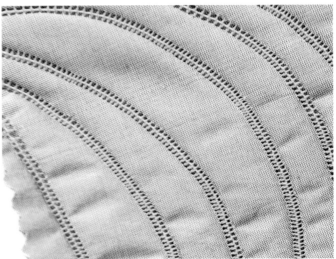

Reverse of fabric.

Tuck and fold

Tuck and fold is an exciting manipulation technique with many possible variations. The technique works best on close-tucked fabric which takes a crease well. These samples are made in shirt-weight cotton.

Prepare the fabric

Make a panel of tucks as Basic Method. Press all the tucks in one direction then all in the other direction, making sure they are all neatly creased and standing proud of the base fabric.

Tuck and fold variation 1

1 Press the tucks all in the same direction, pressing just the very edges. Machine sew in place (lines 1 and 2 on the stitching diagram.

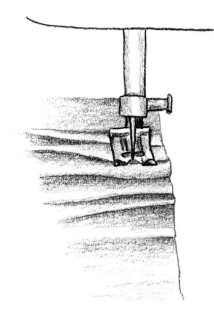

2 Mark a line across the centre of the panel (line 3), then place on the machine with the pleats folding away from you.

The stitching diagram shows the direction and order of stitching; it also shows the direction of the folds when you start.

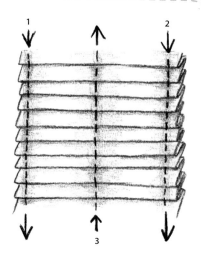

3 Fold over the first pleat and start sewing, folding each pleat as you go. Use a pencil or the tip of a pair of small scissors to hold down each pleat as you come to it.

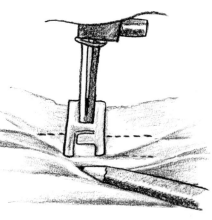

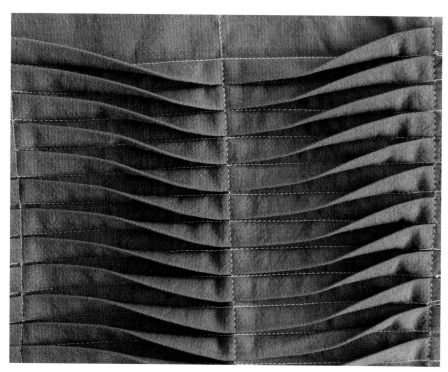

Tuck and fold on plain cotton fabric using contrast stitching.

Tuck and fold variation 2

In this sample, smaller mini-folds have been made between the close stitching at the sides of the panel. The diagram shows the direction and order of stitching.

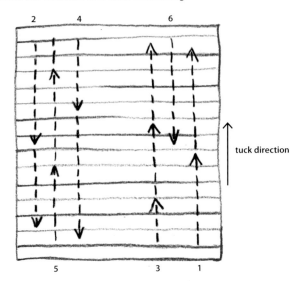

tuck direction

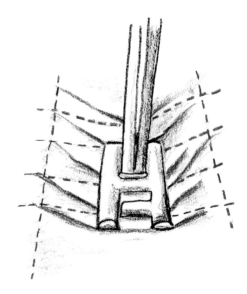

The tucks are folded over so that the edge just meets the stitching, rather than all the way over otherwise the fold would hide the stitching.

Tuck and fold, striped and smocked

The smocked sample is made the same way as Tuck and Fold Variations 1 and 2, but the striped fabric creates a more interesting look. Smocked tucks could also be pressed flat after stitching for a very different effect.

1 Prepare the tucks as described in Prepare the Fabric and press carefully in both directions so the tucks stand up proud from the base fabric.

2 To create the honeycomb smocking effect, the first two tucks are stitched together, just at the very top edge of the fold. To allow the smocking to open up fully, the stitches should be spaced quite widely apart along the length of the fold. These tucks are 3cm (1⅛in) wide and each stripe is 1.5cm (⅝in) wide, so the stitching is done at 6cm (2⅜in) intervals. Mark the first tuck so the stitching points are double the width of the tucks.

3 Knot the thread and insert the needle through the upper pleat first, from bottom to top, then bring the thread over and back through the bottom of the lower fold, so when the stitch is pulled up the knot is enclosed between the two folds.

4 Make two or three stitches close together, then fasten off the thread.

5 Repeat the stitching at the intervals shown in the diagram.

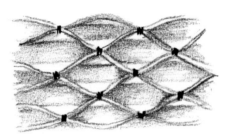

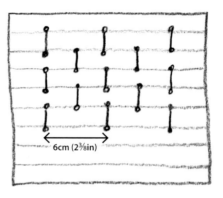

6cm (2⅜in)

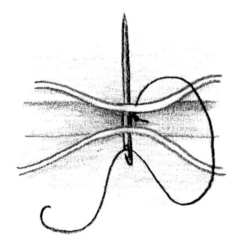

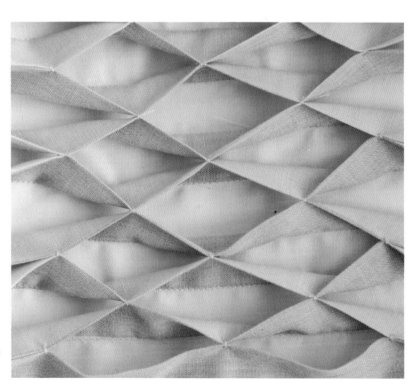

Smocked tucks in striped fabric. This technique works well in plain fabric too.

Ribbon folding

Decorative ribbon work is found in many different cultures and historical periods. Some of the most interesting examples come from India where the technique is traditionally worked in metal ribbon called Gota. Folded ribbon trim is found in dress trimmings and hat decorations, particularly from the early 20th century. Look in museums or books of costume for ideas.

MATERIAL AND DESIGN NOTES

- These techniques work well with heavier ribbon such as grosgrain in silk or rayon.

- True metallic ribbon, as used in India, is hard to get today but it is worth tracking down.

- When working with thick ribbon, it is vital to use sewing clips rather than pins to secure the folds before stitching.

3 Turn the piece over. Fold the long end upwards and to the right so the straight edges meet and the ribbon folds at a 45-degree angle. Clip the new fold.

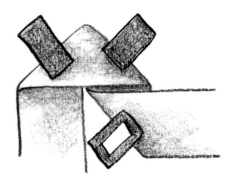

Prairie points

Prairie points are used in patchwork to create a decorative edging and they can be made in a variety of ways. The sample described uses ribbon and is particularly effective with striped ribbon or grosgrain.

4 Fold the long end UNDER and upwards creating a point and a 45-degree angle, and clip.

1 Fold the end over at a 45-degree angle. Clip the fold.

2 Fold the long end over at the same angle so that the straight edges meet, and clip.

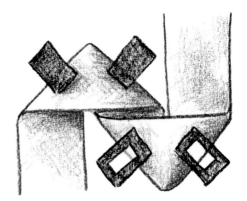

5 Fold the ribbon at a 45-degree angle to the right, and clip.

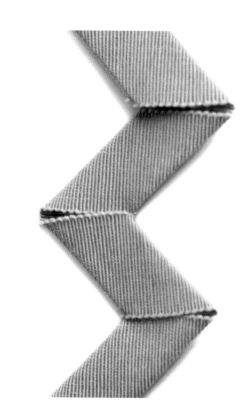

6 Fold the ribbon under and down in the same way. Continue following the same pattern, keeping the piece the same way up from now on.

This technique is reversible so you may consider that this side, the reverse as you make it, is the front.

7 When the ribbon has been folded along its length, keep the clips in place until the work has been pressed to set the folds. Remove each clip one at a time as you press along the length. Alternatively, sew the pleats in place where the edges meet as shown with an 'X' in the diagram.

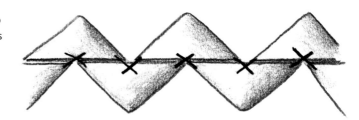

Either side of prairie points folded ribbon can be considered the front. Stitch on whichever side you choose to be the reverse.

Sew and fold prairie points

This technique can also be stitched direct to a base fabric and then folded. First pleat and press the ribbon then position the pleated ribbon trim on the base fabric, ensuring the ribbon is straight and that the base fabric is not puckered (either side of the trim can be the top). Machine sew along the centre line. Fold the pleated ribbon upwards so the points all face in the same direction.

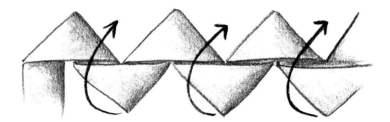

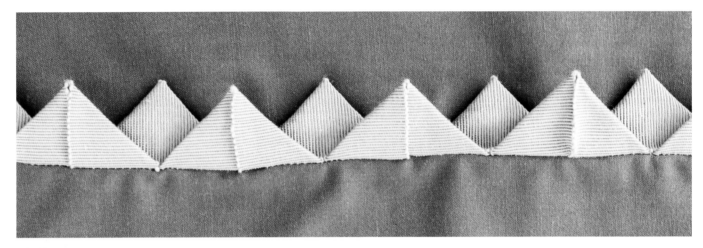

Sew and fold prairie points in vintage grosgrain ribbon which shows the ribbing directions.

Using striped ribbon to make sew and fold prairie points creates an interesting design.

Pointed ribbon fold

This is traditionally used as an edging on Indian textiles. The front and reverse of the ribbon show, so it is best to use a double-faced satin or grosgrain ribbon.

1 Start by folding the ribbon into a V-shape with the folded edge at the bottom, long tail to the left.

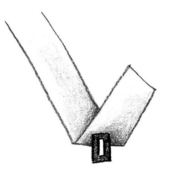

2 Take the long tail, fold it across to the right so the bottom edge is horizontal.

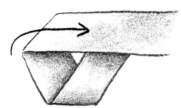

3 Fold the long tail behind and down to create the first triangle. The tail should be hidden behind the first triangle and hang down at the same angle.

4 Loop the tail up under itself so it points upwards and to the left, ready to make the next triangle, and continue from step 2.

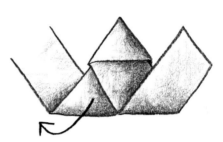

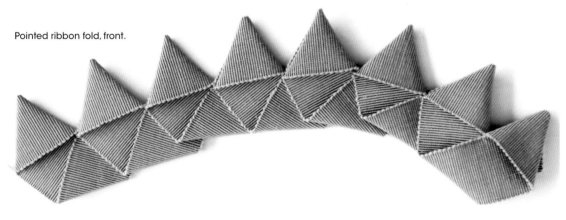

Pointed ribbon fold, front.

5 Sew the triangles together using hand stitching running along the back, making tiny stitches in the valleys between the triangles.

Pointed ribbon fold, reverse.

Arrowhead fold

This design was found used on a 1940s hat trimming, made from grosgrain ribbon. This sample is made in bias binding.

1 Start by folding a triangle at the end of the ribbon, with both lengths pointing down and the long tail on the right side. Clip.

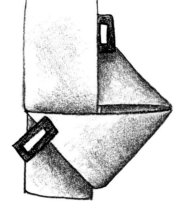

2 Fold the tail across to the left creating a 45-degree angle. Clip the fold.

3 Turn the tail under itself and up to create the other half of the triangle.

4 Flip the triangle that you have just made upwards, bringing the tail out of the way so it points down to give you two triangles on top of each other. Adjust the triangles so that the top triangle is slightly lower than the triangle beneath. Reposition the clips so you have one on each side. (If required you can stitch the triangles together at this point, and directly onto a backing if you choose to.)

5 Fold the ribbon under and towards the right this time, then upwards to create another triangle. Flip the triangle up. Clip, stitch and continue. Press as you go; if pressing does not hold the folds in place, you will need to sew down the folds at each stage, and this may apply if using ribbons that have a lot of spring in them.

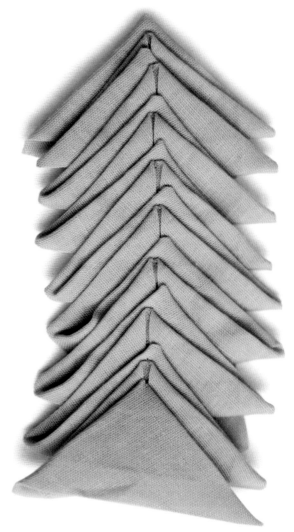

Arrowhead fold: you can sew it onto a backing fabric, another ribbon or straight onto the finished work.

Folded shapes

Single shapes, folded then applied in patterns and tessellations, are endlessly fascinating. This section covers lots of possible designs, but no doubt there are many more for you to discover.

MATERIAL AND DESIGN NOTES

- Changing fabrics will create radically different effects, as will cutting on the bias or straight grain. In many cases raw edges will show, so non-fraying fabrics or tight weaves are useful.

- All the samples shown use squares or circles. Other shapes could be used although the techniques given here are based on shapes that have two-way symmetry, so rectangles for instance, will not work in the same way.

Overlap squares

Cut as many squares as desired from bias-cut or non-fraying fabric – the sample is made in felt. Take one square and place on point (with a corner pointing up, like a diamond). Fold the side corners to the centre and overlap. Stitch by hand through all layers or directly onto the base fabric.

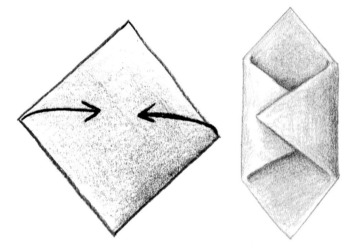

Overlap squares: adjust each square by eye rather than by measuring. Apply in tessellating patterns to a base fabric sewing along the points and through the centres.

Stitched square

1 Cut squares from bias-cut strips. Take a square and fold it so the opposite corners meet. (Fold along the grain if you wish to press the finished shape flat, or against the grain if you want it to retain some 3D shape.)

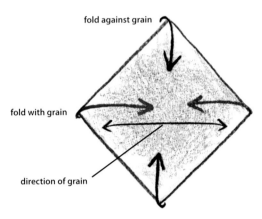

3 Open out and press flat if required. Sew the finished shapes directly onto the background fabric in patterns of your choosing.

Stitched square, unpressed.

Stitched square, pressed.

2 Measure across the folded triangle and divide this measurement by three, then sew the folded triangle together one-third of the way from its point. So if the total width is 6cm (2⅜in), sew together 2cm (¾in) from the point.

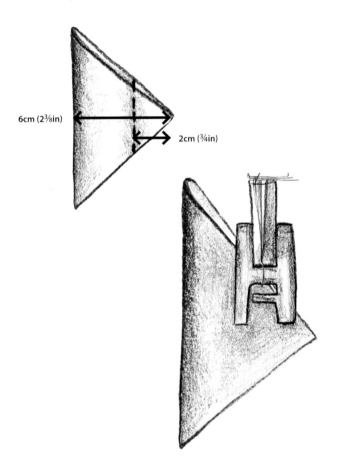

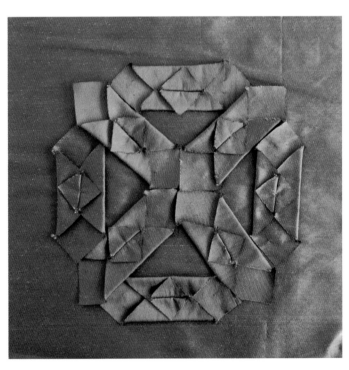

Stitched square, appliqué.

Shawl fold square

Cut squares on the straight grain. Take one square and fold diagonally. Bring the two corners to meet the bottom point. Stitch in place by hand. For the neatest effect, prepare all of the squares before sewing them onto the background fabric.

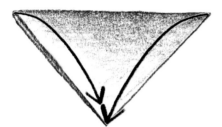

Appliqué tips

Start with the top row; sew in place around the bottom (raw) edge. Position the next row to hide the raw edges and continue. At the end, you may need to stitch through from the back and catch the points down with tiny stitches to stop them flapping around.

Shawl fold square.

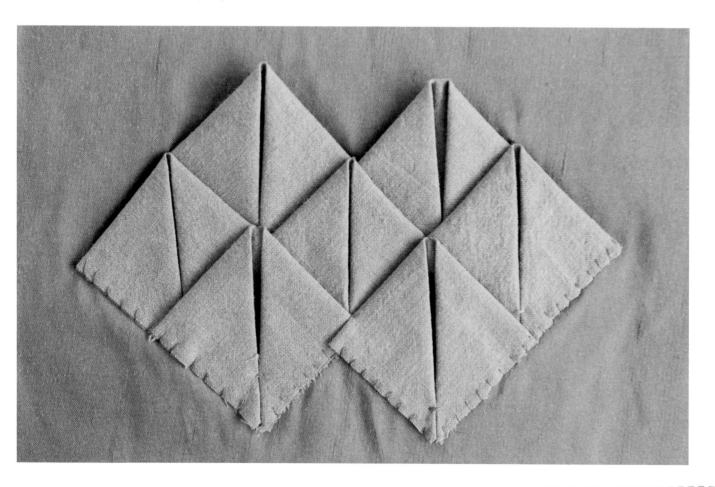

Fold variations for shawl fold

Overlap the edges when you fold for a more 3D effect. Do not press.

Stitch the point down, then fold back the openings and hold with a single stitch.

Contrast shawl fold

Cut two triangles from contrasting fabrics of similar weight, 2cm (¾in) larger than you need. Sew together along the bias edge, and press the seam open. Trim off the points and cut down to the correct size. Fold and press along the sewn line and use to fold Shawl Fold Square.

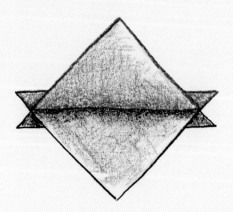

Contrast shawl fold.

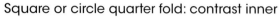

Square or circle quarter fold

Cut squares or circles from non-fraying fabric or bias-cut strips. Fold in half diagonally and then in half again. Sew close to the point so as not to flatten the shape.

Square or circle quarter fold: contrast inner

Cut a smaller square to place inside a larger square. Fold and stitch together as one piece, ensuring the inner fabric is definitely caught by the stitching.

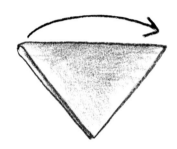

A square quarter fold with contrast inner.

The square quarter fold.

A circle quarter fold with three contrast layers.

The circle quarter fold.

Project Idea:
Ripple Brooch

This felt brooch has been my best seller for years. It is ideally made in recycled wool felt which has a lovely thickness to it. Wool felt is also suitable but cheap craft felt does not work so well at all. Polyester fleece can also be used.

Technique: Circle Quarter Fold
Material: Recycled wool felt or wool felt

- Fold and stitch seven pieces of wool felt using the Circle Quarter Fold technique.

- Cut two extra circles slightly smaller for the backing.

- Apply four of the quarter circles to one of the backing circles, points to centre, and stitch down at points only.

- Stitch the remaining three quarter circles on top, again only stitching the points so they stand up. Trim the edges to make a smooth dome-shape.

- Sew a brooch pin onto the remaining backing circle, then attach to the back of the folded piece, sewing all around the edges, so hiding all the stitching.

Square quarter fold: pinwheel grouping

Make four Square Quarter Folds using wool felt. Cut a backing square the same size, also from felt. Arrange the four quarter squares to make a square so that the folds and the open folds point the same way. Stitch to the backing felt just at the points, and allow the folds to open out.

Square quarter fold: pinwheel grouping.

Trefoil fold

This shape is an interesting variation on a traditional origami fold that works well on fabric.

1 Cut squares on either the straight or bias grain and fold in half diagonally. Fold the sides to the centre as Shawl Fold Square. Press lightly.

2 Unfold the just-folded triangles to lie flat at either side. Holding at the base, put your finger inside the right-hand triangle and lift it up and out so the just-pressed fold line matches up with the fold line underneath to make a kite-shaped fold. Repeat on the left-hand side.

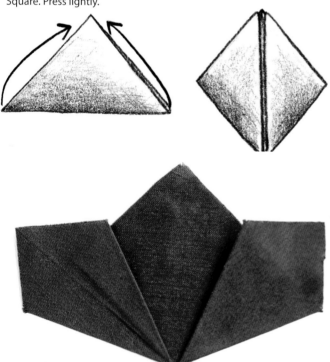

Trefoil fold.

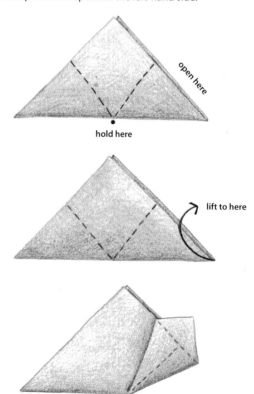

open here

hold here

lift to here

Applied trefoil shapes

Press the trefoils lightly so they retain some 3D shape. Position the shapes as required on the backing fabric, and then stitch down at the points using invisible stitches.

The trefoil shapes are made in crisp organic cotton, a fabric that takes a crease well. These could be applied to a contrasting background too.

Wings and aeroplanes

These folded shapes are a combination of origami folds and folds made for paper aeroplanes. They can be made from bias or straight grain fabric squares, and applied to create dense surface texture.

Wings fold

Fold a square in half diagonally and in half again as for Square Quarter Fold. Sew from the centre of the long side to the point, by hand or machine.

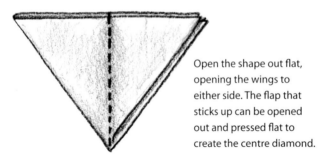

Open the shape out flat, opening the wings to either side. The flap that sticks up can be opened out and pressed flat to create the centre diamond.

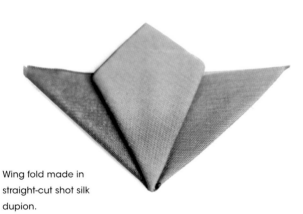

Wing fold made in straight-cut shot silk dupion.

Pinched wings

Make the Wings Fold but make sure you use bias grain squares. For pinched wings do not press the flap flat when you have opened it out; instead bring the two sides of the flap (points A and B) together to create the shape. Sew together with tiny stitches through all layers.

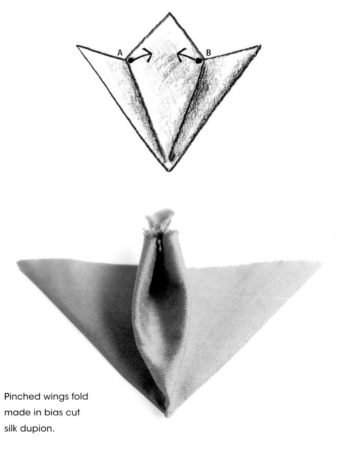

Pinched wings fold made in bias cut silk dupion.

Aeroplane fold

1 Fold a square in half diagonally. Fold one side over and hold in place with a sewing clip.

Aeroplane fold.

2 Fold the folded over side back on itself so the fold lies on the centre line – like a paper aeroplane – and clip.

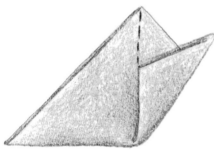

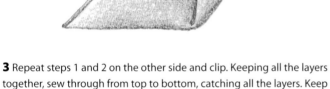

Aeroplane fold, pressed.

3 Repeat steps 1 and 2 on the other side and clip. Keeping all the layers together, sew through from top to bottom, catching all the layers. Keep the stitches small so the wings can spring back up.

Aeroplane fold grouping: apply six aeroplanes to a circular backing, points to the centre.

The circle aeroplane fold is made in the same way as the Aeroplane Fold; this sample is left unpressed and not stitched in place.

Circle thirds fold

This technique is tricky to master. You might want to try it with a large paper circle first and mark the lines and letters on.

1 Cut circles from medium-weight fabric, at least 7–8cm (2¾– 3⅛in) diameter. Fold in half to create a semi-circle then into quarters and press lightly to create a slight centre crease. Unfold to a semi circle. Follow the diagram and mark each quarter of the semi-circle with a line or a mark on the edge.

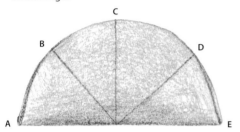

2 Work the left side first. Fold point A to point D and finger press or clip in place.

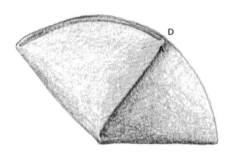

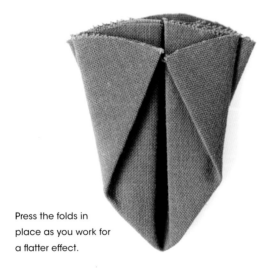

Press the folds in place as you work for a flatter effect.

3 Fold A back so it creases on the centre line and overlaps on the left side.

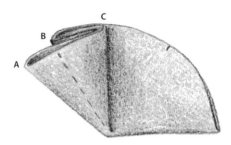

4 Bring the overlapping point A back to the centre fold but slightly down from the raw edge (see photos of finished samples also).

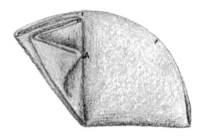

5 Make the other side folds by folding E so it just overlaps the folds you have already made, roughly to the point marked X. Fold back along the centre line then fold point E to the centre, to match with point A.

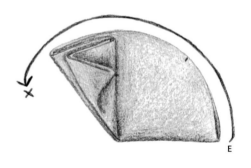

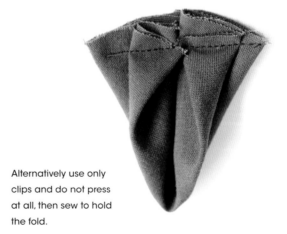

Alternatively use only clips and do not press at all, then sew to hold the fold.

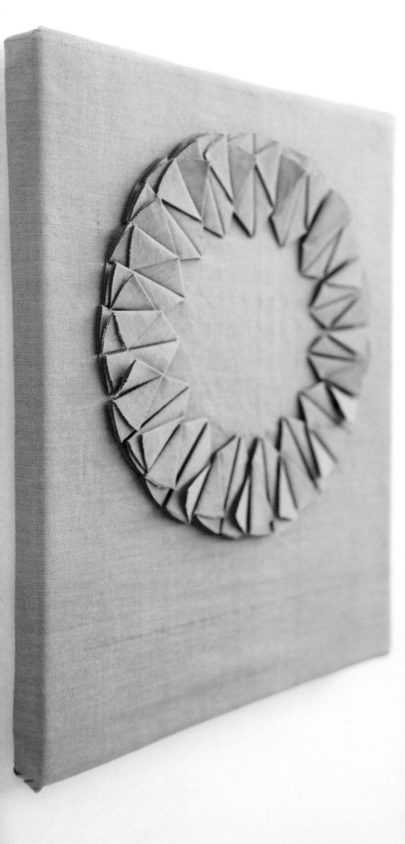

Project Idea:
Aeroplane Fold Wall Panel

This piece is an exercise in optical illusion. At first look, the pleats appear to be made from the base fabric, whereas they are really sewn onto a matching fabric, merely creating an impression of serious complexity.

Technique: Aeroplane Fold Pressed
Material: Organic or plain weave shirt-weight cotton

• Make 15 (or as many as desired) folded circles using the Aeroplane Fold technique.

• Cut matching backing fabric and use a circle template to arrange the folded shapes into a circle, points facing in.

• You will find that the folded shapes do not butt up to each other completely, so experiment to find an arrangement that works. More folded circles will create a larger circle, and fewer a smaller circle.

• Sew the folded circles in place just at the points and at the outside raw edge.

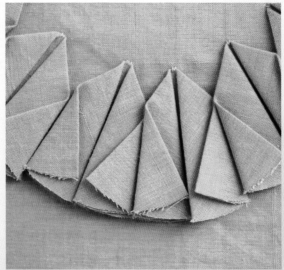

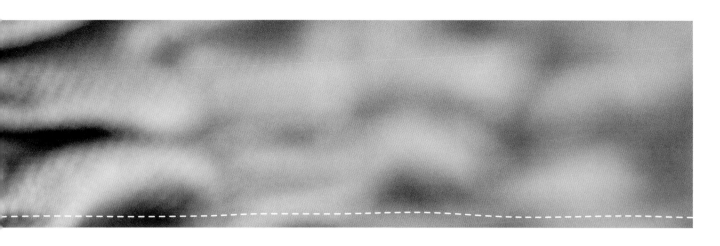

Stitch & Gather

Ruffles and frills basics

Frills, gathers and ruffles can be used as trimmings in the traditional way, or inset into fabrics to create a heavily-textured look. They can be massed to cover fabric completely or applied in swooping curves. Material choice, fabric grain and edge finish will make a huge difference to how a ruffle or frill looks, and whether you use a machine or hand gathering technique will play a part too.

MATERIAL AND DESIGN NOTES

- Heavy fabrics will only gather a small amount, whereas fine fabrics such as chiffon will gather to almost nothing.

- A crisper, stiff fabric such as unwashed silk dupion will hold its shape well, whereas soft fabrics can flop.

- Thick fabrics work best on the bias and gathered with large stitches.

Exploring options

The following samples, all made with unwashed silk dupion, show how you cut the fabric strip (on the straight grain or on the bias) and how you finish the edges of the fabric strip (or not) will have an effect on the look of the ruffle you make. Using bias-cut fabric eliminates the need for hemming or edge finishes but the ruffle will behave very differently to a straight cut piece of fabric.

Raw edge, straight grain: the soft, frayed edge can be very attractive, and a single line of stitching approx 3mm (⅛in) from the edge will limit the fraying.

Narrow hem, straight grain: the thickness created by the hem fold adds structure to the edge.

Zigzagged edge, straight grain: a narrow zigzag wraps and finishes the edge for a softer finish than hemming.

Bias-cut, unhemmed: a bias ruffle tends to curve and the gathers can have a pronounced diagonal look, but it has a nice soft edge and gathers beautifully.

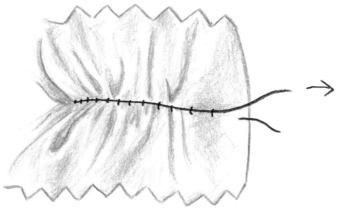

Pinked, straight grain: cutting the strip with pinking shears will reduce fraying, yet still leaves a soft, decorative edge.

Machine gathering

Standard machine gathers

Use this technique for longer lengths of gathering with softer, finer fabrics (the machine stitches produce very fine gathers which do not work in very thick fabrics). Always use a strong thread such as good quality polyester.

1 Set the machine to the longest stitch length. Fasten firmly at the start of sewing. Stitch the full length of the ruffle, then remove from the machine without fastening off leaving long tails. Using a pin, loosen the bobbin thread at the end.

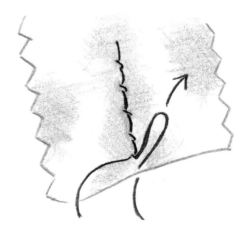

2 Begin to gently pull the bobbin thread, sliding the gathers along the fabric.

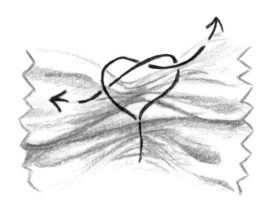

3 Once the ruffle is the desired length, tie the two threads together firmly or sew in the ends.

Standard machine gathered ruffle.

Using a gathering foot

It is possible to create gathers on the machine by stitching with a long stitch length and high tension (8–9), but there is always a risk that the thread may snap. If you use a gathering foot, however, this risk is limited (see Tool Guide). A gathering foot also allows you to gather the edge of a ruffle and sew it direct to a straight piece of fabric at the same time.

Using a ruffler foot

A ruffler foot attachment can be used to produce tiny pleats that look more like fine gathers (see Pleat & Fold: Knife Pleats for more information). Set the foot so it pleats at every stitch and adjust the pleat length screw to change the depth of the pleat to suit the fabric and the effect you require.

Ruffler foot gathers: this sample has relatively deep pleats and uses a lot of fabric.

Hand-stitched gathering

Stitching by hand gives you more control and allows you to adjust the size of the gathers by the length of the stitches you use, as illustrated in the samples shown.

1 Knot a strong thread firmly. Sew along the edge or centre of the fabric using running stitch.

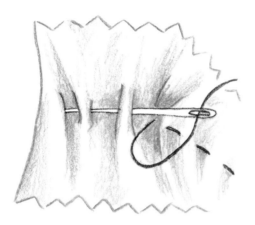

2 Leaving the needle attached, pull up the thread, adjusting the gathers to be tight or loose as required.

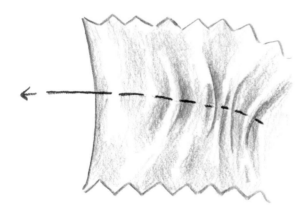

3 Once you are happy with the look of your gathers, sew in the thread to hold them in place.

Note: When gathering a long piece of fabric, start sewing from the middle outwards, leaving very, very long tails. When you reach the edge, return to the middle and rethread the needle with the long tails to sew the other side. Remember to fasten in one end before you pull the thread up.

Hand-stitched gathers using small stitches approx 2mm (³⁄₃₂in) long.

Hand-stitched gathers using stitches 3mm (⅛in) long – longer stitches create deeper ruffles.

Hand-stitched gathers using stitches 8mm (⁵⁄₁₆in) long – very long stitches work well with thicker fabrics or to create fewer, deeper gathers.

Ruffle variations

There are many ways to vary the basic ruffle techniques described in the last section to create different textures and different shapes. The samples shown here use bias-cut fabric which curves distinctively. Ribbon or hemmed straight-grain fabric would behave somewhat differently.

MATERIAL AND DESIGN NOTES

- Fine fabrics have much more flexibility for manipulations such as centre tuck gathers, or for double-edge gathers.

- When working on wide strips of fabric, you could use different gathering techniques along each edge; for example, pleating along one edge and fine gathers along the other.

- Most of the ruffles shown use stitching in a straight line. Different effects can be created by stitching in zigzag and other patterns.

- To attach gathers to fabric, make the gathering stitching first, then pin, tack (baste) and sew along the gathering line so the stitching is invisible.

Single edge gathers

Gathering along one edge of the fabric produces a frill or ruffle suitable for attaching to another piece of fabric. Stitch about 5mm (¼in) from the edge of the ruffle, or further in if the fabric is likely to fray.

Bias-cut ruffles stitched along one edge will produce a curved piece, which can be used to make rosette forms and undulating ruffles. Stitch as described for Single Edge Gathers.

Centre tuck gathers

This is effective in fine fabrics such as silk or chiffon. Fold the fabric strip in half and then make the gathering stitch 5mm (¼in) from the folded edge, using hand or machine gathering methods. (*Note:* The ruffler foot method is not suitable.) Unfold the ruffle to reveal the centre tuck.

Double edge gathers

Both edges of the fabric can be gathered to produce a ruched strip. This can be applied with the raw edges showing, or inset into fabric to hide the stitching. This works well with fine to medium fabrics, either bias-cut or straight grain. Gather using any machine or hand gathering technique.

Curved double edge gathers

In this sample, a bias-cut strip is gathered along both edges, then one edge is pulled tighter than the other to create a pronounced curve. Longer strips can be manipulated to create S-shape curves and interesting undulating shapes.

This technique is most effective on bias-cut fabric, but straight grain can work too. To enable you to manipulate the gathers, you will need to gather with long machine stitching or hand stitching. *Note:* The gathering foot or ruffler foot methods will not allow you to adjust the gathers.

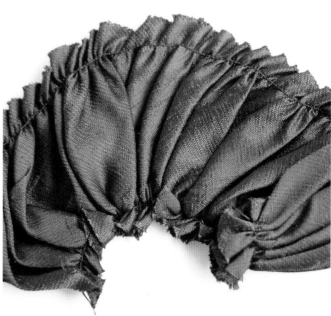

Double stitched flat ruffle

In this sample a double row of gathers is sewn 1.5cm (⅝in) apart to create a flatter ruffle, which is ideal for applying onto a background fabric. This photograph shows the reverse so you can see the gathering threads.

Shaped fabric ruffle

Ruffles can also be made with fabric that has been cut into undulating or zigzag shapes, and stitched along its centre.

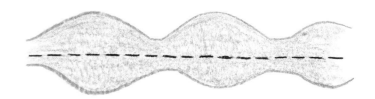

Layered ruffle

This is most effective in light bias-cut fabrics although lightly fraying or pinked straight-grain will also work, as will lightweight ribbon. Layer the fabrics up then tack (baste) through the centre before gathering, to prevent the layers from shifting.

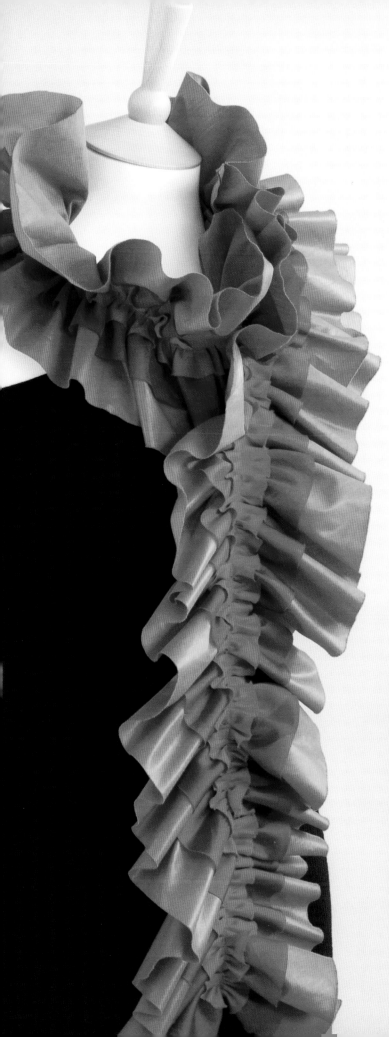

Project Idea:
Ruffle scarf

This scarf is made from three lengths of bias-cut fabric, each three times longer than the finished scarf length.

Technique: Layered Ruffle
Material: Base layer – crisp cotton, unwashed silk dupion or other crisp, lightweight fabric; middle and top layers – silk chiffon or satin, habotai silk, synthetics, silk dupion or any soft fabric (for a scarf measuring 1.5m [approx 60in] you will need 4.5m [5yd] long strips of each fabric).

• Cut bias strips of fabric and join to make long lengths of the following widths: for the base layer 25cm (10in) wide; for the middle layer 15cm (6in) wide; for the top layer 8cm (3in) wide.

• Layer the fabrics and pin in place. Hand or machine tack (baste) along the centre to hold the layers together. Sew gathering stitching along the centre: use a ruffler foot if the fabrics are not too thick, or machine gathering, or hand-stitched gathering.

• If working by hand, start in the middle of the scarf and sew towards one end, leaving the thread attached to the spool. Fasten the end, then cut enough of the remaining thread off the spool to sew to the other end, before pulling up. Use a very strong thread and pull up carefully so you don't snap it.

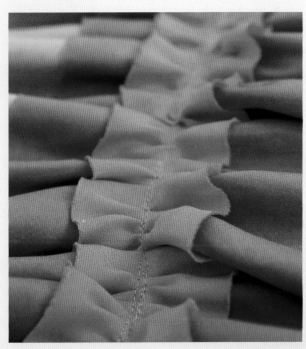

Pattern stitched ribbon ruffles

This hand-stitching technique uses running stitches in patterns along the ribbon or fabric to create scalloped edges. It is traditionally worked on silk ribbon to be used as a trimming or coiled into fabric flowers. It works well on a soft medium to wide ribbon. The samples shown have been made on 3cm (1⅛in) wide cotton bias binding (unfolded), which is quite stiff.

1 The design can be drawn onto the ribbon using vanishing pen or other marking method if preferred or worked directly onto the ribbon freehand.

2 Knot a strong, matching colour thread and fasten at one end of the ribbon. Follow the illustrations for stitching guidelines for your chosen pattern and make small stitches about 3mm (⅛in) long.

3 When the stitching is complete, draw up the gathers and adjust as required before fastening the thread off firmly. Do not press. (*Note:* If you run out of thread as you work, draw up the gathers, fasten and continue with a new length of thread.)

Zigzag-stitched ribbon ruffle

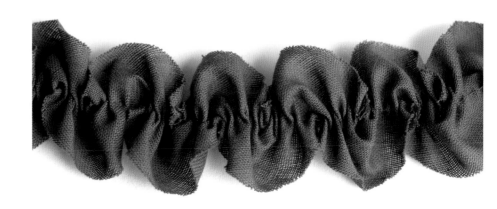

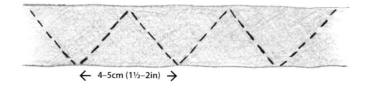

← 4–5cm (1½–2in) →

Curve-stitched ribbon ruffle

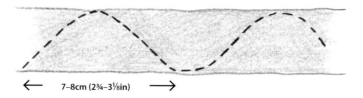

← 7–8cm (2¾–3⅛in) →

Squares-stitched ribbon ruffle

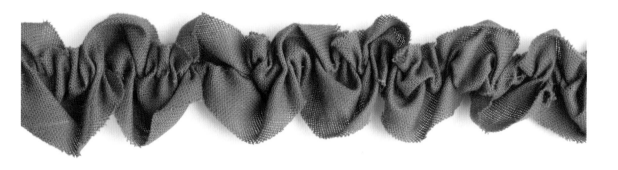

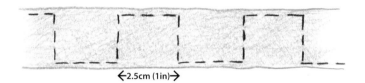

←2.5cm (1in)→

Peaks-stitched ribbon ruffle

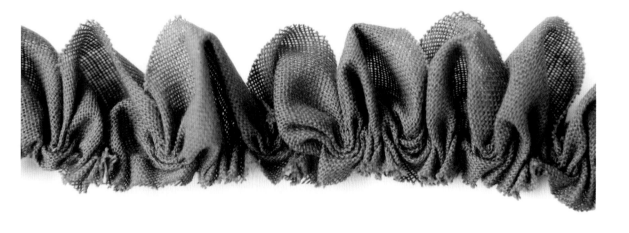

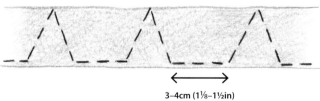

3–4cm (1⅛–1½in)

Shirring and decorative gathering

The gathering methods described in this section can be used to create larger pieces of fabric covered in gathers and manipulations, or as decorative elements to shape a larger piece of garment fabric, such as shirring on a dress bodice.

MATERIAL AND DESIGN NOTES

- Wide-sleeved 19th century dresses sometimes use narrow rows of shirring at the top of the sleeve, with the fabric billowing at the elbow as the shirring is released. Random gathers could be used in a similar way to create a more contemporary look.

- Fine fabrics are ideal for shirring although heavier fabrics can also be shirred, ideally by hand to manage the fabric thickness.

- Sheer fabrics could be shirred using coloured shirring elastic or contrasting thread to create interesting effects.

Hand-stitched techniques

These techniques use hand stitching which enables you to have lots of control over the shaping and structuring of the gathers. Hand-stitched gathers are ideal for thick or heavy fabrics – use a strong thread, firm knots and large stitches. Different effects can be produced by varying how tight you pull the thread to gather the fabric.

Straight row gathers

This technique is the basis for English Smocking and creates long, narrow folds or tubes. At least two rows of gathering stitches are required for even gathers, and the stitching must be regular to produce evenly spaced tubes of a consistent size. Your stitch length determines how big or deep the gathers are, for example larger stitches spaced widely apart create deep ridge and furrow effects typical of smocking. This technique will only work on straight-grain fabric; bias-cut fabric will not form into tubes in the same way.

1 Mark the fabric with evenly spaced dots using vanishing pen or other marking method. The rows must be aligned correctly with the second row directly beneath the first row. For the sample shown the dots are placed 1cm (⅜in) apart.

2 Use a strong thread and stitch it in firmly at the start of the first row of dots. Sew running stitches along the row, going in at one dot and out at the next. Complete the row by leaving long thread tails at the end. Sew along the second row of marked dots in the same way, again leaving long thread tails at the end.

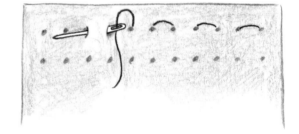

3 Pull both sets of threads up together, spreading out the gathers evenly. Use a pencil to stroke the fabric tubes into place.

4 Reattach the needle and sew in the ends; alternatively, knot the pairs of threads together. Then steam well to help set the gathers.

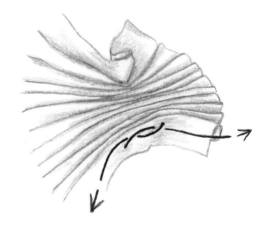

Straight row gathers.

Irregular straight row gathers.

Irregular straight row gathers

This technique creates a highly textured surface. Experiment with different fabrics: thick fabrics, such as the heavy linen used for the sample, won't pull that tightly, whereas fine silk will shrink to almost nothing. Stitching in the direction of the bias rather than the straight grain will produce different effects again.

1 Use a strong thread and stitch it in firmly at the start of your first line of stitching. Work a straight line of running stitch using random-sized stitches. Work rows 1–3cm (⅜–1⅛in) apart depending on the thickness of the fabric and the effect you want to achieve.

2 Pull up the threads and gently slide the gathers down the fabric, taking care not snap any threads. Adjust the gathers as required, then fasten the threads as described for Straight Row Gathers.

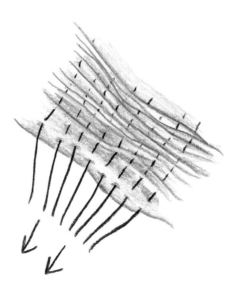

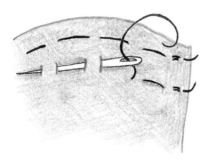

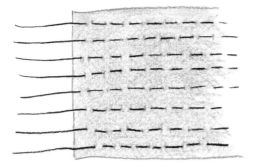

Random line gathers

Lines of running stitch are made across the fabric at random, then pulled up, some tighter, some looser. The diagram shows possible lines of stitching but this is entirely experimental. Varying the length of the stitches used will also create different effects as the gathers produced will also be varied.

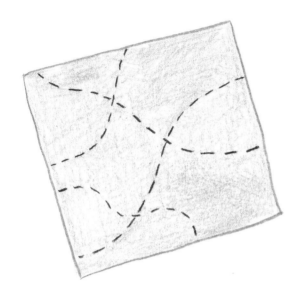

Random line gathers using shirt-weight cotton (thick fabrics will not gather up so tightly).

Random line gathers made in light fabric, then pressed and steamed thoroughly to flatten.

Zigzag shirring

This is exactly the same technique as used for the Zigzag-Stitched Ribbon Ruffle (see Ruffle Variations: Pattern Stitched Ribbon Ruffles), but worked across a large piece of fabric. Thick fabrics that will hold the shapes are most effective for this technique. Finer fabrics may need a double layer, interlining with silk organza or backing with iron-on interfacing. Although the zigzag variation is described, any of the patterns used for the Pattern Stitched Ribbon Ruffles work just as well.

1 Working on the back of the fabric, mark two rows approx 5cm (2in) apart. Draw in the zigzag lines between the rows leaving 5cm (2in) between each point. You can alter these measurements to make your zigzags any size.

2 Stitch the marked zigzag lines with long running stitch about 6–8mm (¼–⁵⁄₁₆in) long. Use strong, doubled thread as this technique creates a lot of tension.

3 Draw up the stitching and distribute the gathers as desired, then sew in the thread firmly.

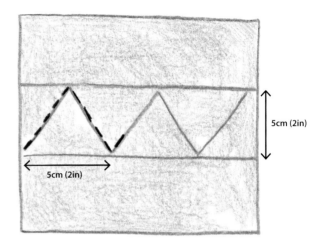

5cm (2in)

5cm (2in)

Thick cotton velvet creates a dense, luxurious effect when stitched in zigzag shirring.

Machine shirring

Three different machine techniques can be used to create dense gathering or shirring on fabric. For the samples shown, the stitching was worked freehand, although if you prefer you can draw guidelines on the fabric, but be aware that, as you will be working with the right side of the fabric facing up, the lines may show. Alternatively, you could also use a quilting guide – a metal bar that attaches to the side of the sewing machine foot (see Tool Guide). Shirred fabric is inclined to curl, particularly elasticated shirring.

Stitch and pull

This technique is the same as creating a basic ruffle using standard machine gathers. A long stitch length is used, combined with high tension (if this does not snap the thread), and the bobbin thread is pulled up. For the sample shown, a lightweight fabric (vintage rayon) was used and strong thread.

1 Mark the fabric on the right side if desired. Fasten the thread firmly and sew across the fabric using long stitches, leaving long thread tails at the end of sewing.

2 Work the next and subsequent rows following the guidelines, or using the edge of the machine foot as a guide. (For the sample, the rows were stitched 7mm–1cm [approx ⅜in] apart, judged by eye.) Remember to leave long thread tails at the end of each row for sewing in.

3 Pull up the bobbin threads and ease the gathers as much as required. To fasten, use a hand-sewing needle to sew in the thread tails, or knot pairs together if possible.

Gathering foot

Whereas Stitch and Pull gathering can be adjusted to suit after finishing the stitching, shirring made with a gathering foot cannot be adjusted once sewn. This, however, makes it much less vulnerable to coming undone, which is useful in garments. Working with the gathering foot produces a medium density of shirring as shown in the sample. Use guidelines or work freehand when stitching the rows, and reverse at the beginning and end of each row to fasten.

Stitch and pull machine shirring.

Machine shirring with gathering foot.

Shirring elastic

The fastest way to make shirred fabric is to use shirring elastic in the sewing machine bobbin. This is the technique used to make shirred or faux-smocked summer dresses. There are endless variations on how you stitch to create a wide range of effects and a selection are explained below and overleaf. This technique works best on fine, floppy fabrics such as silk/viscose velvet, lightweight cotton lawn, fine habotai silk, and chiffon.

1 Wind shirring elastic onto the bobbin by hand using a little tension, but do not pull it tight. For the top thread, use a polyester thread rather than a cotton thread as it is stronger under tension. Choose a colour to match your fabric.

2 Mark guidelines onto the fabric if required. Place the fabric right side up on the machine. Set a long straight stitch length (experiment to find the best length for each fabric) and fasten the thread by reversing at the start.

3 Sew along the marked lines or work freehand if you prefer. When sewing the second and subsequent rows, you will need to stretch out the fabric as you sew, so you have a smooth flat fabric to stitch.

4 Reverse to fasten at the end of each row. Alternatively, sew in a continuous line, lifting the presser foot to turn the fabric.

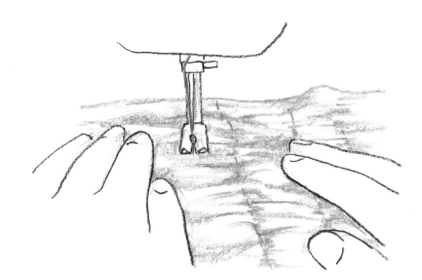

Silk dupion gathered using shirring elastic stitched along the warp threads (vertically to the weave) rather than the weft, as the warp has more flexibility.

Shirring effects

Shirring can be manipulated to create varied effects. Each of these techniques will look radically different in thicker or softer fabric. Some are made using a gathering foot while others work best with elastic, but experimentation will generate more variations.

Spaced shirring

This sample, worked on shot rayon taffeta, has spaced out rows of gathers made using a gathering foot.

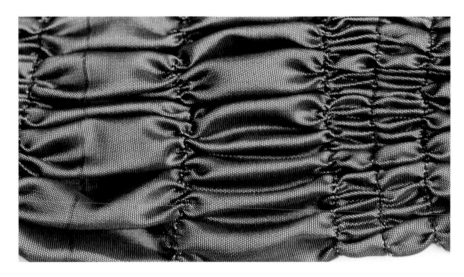

Spaced shirring.

Puffed shirring

In this sample a widely spaced shirring fabric length is sewn to a base cloth, which allows for further manipulation of the shirred fabric to create a puffed effect.

1 Sew rows of shirring at about 6cm (2⅜in) apart along the fabric length. Flatten out and pin the shirred fabric onto the base fabric.

2 Sew across the first row of shirring using large stitches to anchor the shirred fabric to the base fabric.

3 Manipulate the shirred fabric so the next row of shirring is close to the first to create a puffed effect. Sew across the shirring as in step 2 to anchor the puffs, and continue making regular or irregular puffs.

3cm (1⅛in)   5cm (2in)   4.5cm (1¾in)

Puffed shirring with irregular puffs. The left-hand section is 3cm (1⅛in) – half the distance between the shirring lines; the middle section is spaced at 5cm (2in) and the right-hand side section is 4.5cm (1¾in), for slightly more puffing.

Tucked shirring

Tucks can be combined with shirring to create heavily textured effects. This works best on fine fabrics such as light silk crepe or chiffon. The sample was created using the gathering foot.

1 The tuck and the shirring are created in one step. Each tuck is a total of 2cm (¾in) wide and they can be spaced 1.5cm (⅝in) apart or wider as preferred. To prepare the fabric mark from right to left, starting 5cm (2in) in. First mark the 2cm (¾in) tuck lines, then 1.5cm (⅝in) gaps, then another set of 2cm (¾in) tuck lines and continue in this way to the end of the fabric.

2 Fold the fabric back on itself, wrong sides together, to create a small fold. With the fold to the right of the sewing machine gathering foot, sew 1cm (⅜in) in from the fold allowing the fabric to gather.

3 Make the next fold and continue, making sure the previous gathers are not caught up as you sew

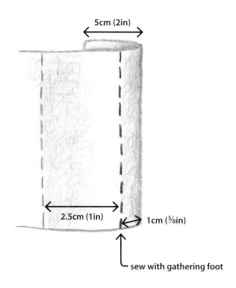

5cm (2in)

2.5cm (1in)

1cm (⅜in)

sew with gathering foot

Tucked shirring: in this sample, the right-hand side tucks are 1.5cm (⅝in) apart and the left one is 2.5cm (1in).

Close-worked shirring

In this sample fine silk fabric has been shirred in close rows just 8mm (5⁄16in) apart. The fabric has shrunk by approx 60 per cent, from 11cm (4¼in) to 4cm (1½in) wide, and the finished fabric has a natural curl.

Close worked shirring worked with matching thread.

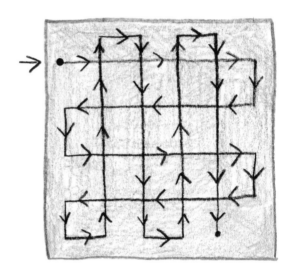

Grid shirring

Rows of shirring elastic are stitched in a grid pattern to create puffed boxes. The stitching lines are worked in a continuous line as shown in the diagram (3cm/1⅛in apart in the sample shown). As this technique is worked with the top of the fabric uppermost on the machine, it is best to mark guidelines with a vanishing pen, or to judge the lines by eye. When working the second rows, keep the fabric stretched as you work.

Grid shirring worked on lightweight silk.

Spiral shirring

The stitching starts in the centre and works outwards in a freehand spiral. The lines of stitching are about 1cm (⅜in) apart.

Spiral shirring.

Applied gathering

Cords and curtain tape can be sewn to fabric to create closely controlled gathers, which in most cases can be made so they are adjustable, allowing the finished piece to be interactive. This is very effective for garments where the look can be changed by releasing or tightening the gathers.

MATERIAL AND DESIGN NOTES

- Curtain tape will show through fine fabrics. Semi-sheer tape designed for net curtains can be used instead. Curtain tape can also be dyed to match the fabric.

- Rows of corded gathers could be applied to fabric in even or random arrangements and then gathered, some tight and some loose, to create a very deeply textured fabric.

- Elastic cord can also be used in place of cord for the hem channel gathers.

Corded gathers

Gathers can be pulled up with piping cord or other thick yarn instead of sewing thread. A channel needs to be created for the cord to pass through, much the same as for drawstring trousers, and this can be done in several ways.

Hem channel

For a gathered edge, the fabric is folded over like a hem to create a small channel through which the piping cord or yarn is threaded. The cord/yarn is fastened at one end and pulled through from the other to create the gathers. This technique is traditionally used on necklines and more recently on pockets to create shape and depth. A cord channel can also be created by sewing fabric strips, such as bias binding, to the back or front of the fabric, through which the cord can be threaded.

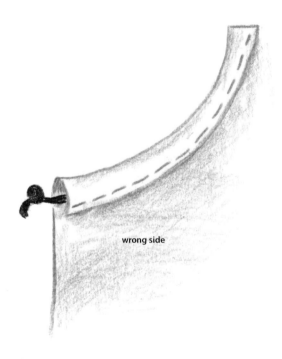

wrong side

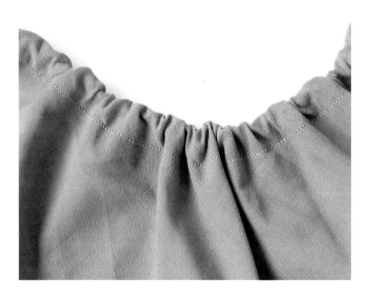

Hem channel: right side of fabric.

Zigzag corded channel

Narrow corded gathers can be created by using zigzag stitch over fine cotton or other strong yarn.

Knot the yarn and place the knotted end at the top end of the line, using pins to hold it in place. Set a wide zigzag stitch and sew along the cord, making sure the stitching is wide enough not to catch the cord in the stitching. Pull the cord to create the gathers, and knot or sew in the end as required.

Double layer channel

Two layers of fabric are sewn together sandwiching the cord between them; this ensures the channel is neat and the gathers are tight. Any size of piping cord can be used for this technique: thicker cord will suit thick fabrics but the effects will vary so experimentation is necessary. You will need a piping or zip foot to get the stitching close to the cord; or stitch by hand.

1 Mark the cord position on the inside (wrong side) of the backing fabric. Place the cord on top, then carefully lay the top fabric over, right side facing up, making sure you have sufficient cord at either end to tie in a knot or sew in. Pin through the fabric layers, without moving the cord, to keep the cord in position.

2 If sewing by hand, work running stitch or backstitch close to the cord along one side, then the other. If sewing by machine, fit the zip or piping foot and adjust the needle so that it is as close to the cord as possible. Sew the right-hand side first, then flip over and sew the other side.

3 Sew in one end or tie a large knot. Pull up the other end, adjust the gathers as required, then knot or sew in the cord to hold the gathers.

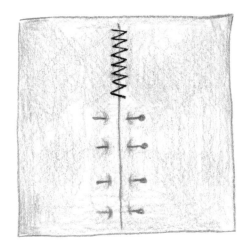

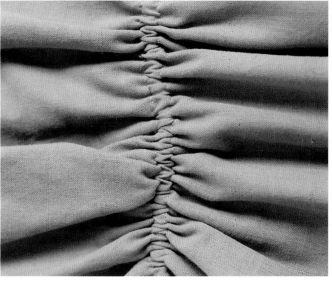

Zigzag corded channel.

Double layer channel.

Curtain tape gathers

Quick and easy gathering can be achieved using ordinary curtain tape sewn onto the reverse side of the fabric. Curtain tape is available in a range of styles, from basic gathers to smocked and box pleated. The samples shown use the basic, narrow tape (2.5cm/1in) designed for lightweight or net curtains. As with other types of gathering, tapes can be pulled up tight or loose, or both when two pieces are sewn on.

1 Cut the tape to the full length of the fabric to be gathered adding approx 4cm (1½in) for turning under at the ends.

2 Fold the ends under, ensuring the strings are tucked in at one end and left free at the other.

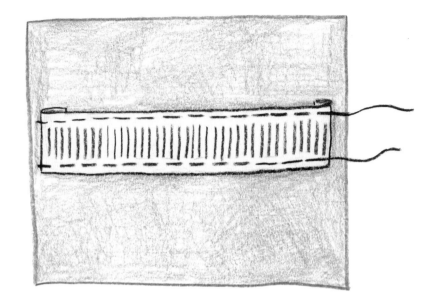

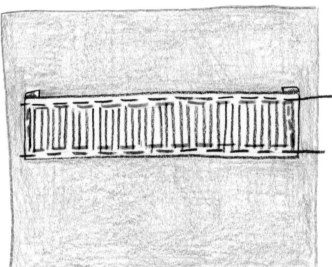

3 Pin in place, then sew all round the edge, avoiding catching the strings at the open end. Pivot at the corners making sure you sew through all the layers. The bobbin thread will show on the right side, so make sure it matches your fabric.

4 Pull the strings gently to make sure they are fixed at the sewn-in end, and if they are not, sew in firmly by hand. Pull up to create the gathers and adjust as required. Tie the strings and cut off the excess; or leave the excess to allow adjustment of the gathers.

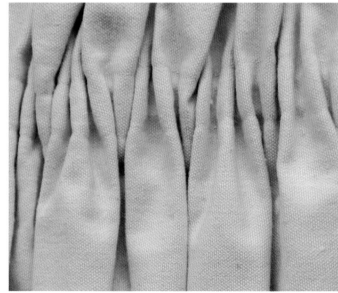

Spaced rows of 2.5cm (1in) tape on heavy canvas.

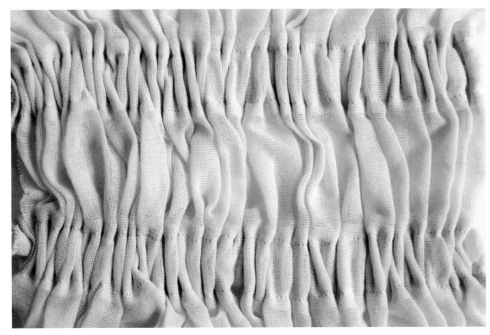

Two rows of 2.5cm (1in) tape worked 3cm (1⅛in) apart on light cotton voile.

One row of 2.5cm (1in) tape sewn in a curving line across medium-weight herringbone linen.

Suffolk puffs

Suffolk puffs are gathered circles of fabric traditionally used as a type of patchwork and particularly common in the 19th century. The puffs are usually made quite small from cotton, but all kinds of fabric can be used, and the shape can be varied for creative effect.

MATERIAL AND DESIGN NOTES

- Lightweight cotton lawn is a good fabric to use for smaller puffs.

- Thick fabrics will only make large puffs, as the gathers are too bulky to make small ones.

- Fine fabrics such as chiffon gather up too much and do not make very successful puffs.

- Some people find that as they stitch the puff works itself inside out. If this is the case for you, you will need to turn it right side out before finishing it off.

Basic method

1 Cut a circle of fabric slightly larger than twice the desired size of the finished puff.

2 Using a doubled and knotted thread, secure the knot on one edge of the fabric circle so it will be concealed in the hem. Fold over the hem edge and work a medium-sized running stitch, continuing to fold over the edge as you go.

3 Continue stitching all the way around the circle keeping the stitches evenly spaced and not too small.

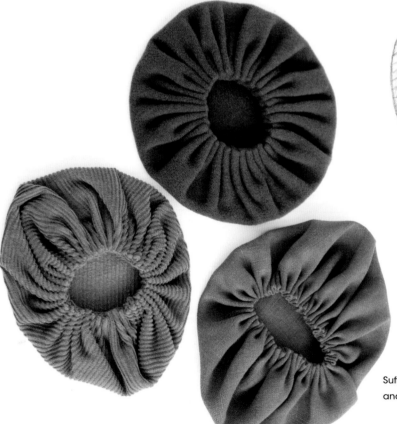

Suffolk puffs: top, round; left, irregular; and right, oval..

4 When you reach your start point, put the needle back through the first stitch so it ends up on the inside of the puff. Start to pull up the stitching, easing the stitches around. Turn the puff right side out if necessary.

5 Once you have pulled the puff to the size you want it to be, secure the thread with several small stitches on the inside of the hem, making sure it is really secure before cutting. To even out the pleats, pull the edges while holding the middle of the puff.

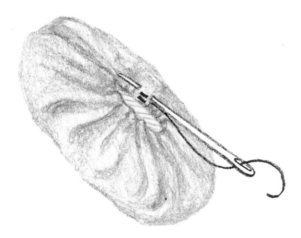

Shape variations

Oval or irregular
Make these following the Basic Method, but start with an oval or irregular shaped piece of fabric.

Square or rectangular
The technique for these varies slightly from the Basic Method as square or rectangular-shaped puffs have little peaks of excess fabric in the corners.

1 Cut a square or rectangle of fabric slightly more than twice the desired finished size.

2 Press the corners in on the wrong side by taking a fold approx 1cm (⅜in) long.

3 Work as Basic Method, steps 2 and 3, stitching around the folded corners as shown in the diagram.

4 Complete as Basic Method, steps 4 and 5.

A square puff: thicker fabrics, like the velvet sample shown, work best as larger puffs and need large stitches to create good centre gathers.

Contrast centre

A coloured centre can be added to any style of Suffolk puff to create a contrast lining. The lining fabric also acts as a stiffener, creating a sturdier puff. There are two methods for adding a contrast centre, by using fusible fabric or by tacking (basting) the fabric in place.

Tacked (basted) lining

The method described is for making a circular contrast centre but this will work for any shape variation of the puff – just cut the lining fabric to the same shape at the puff you are making.

1 Cut a circle of lining fabric approx 5mm (¼in) less than half the diameter of the main fabric. So if the puff fabric is 20cm (8in) diameter, the lining should be 9.5cm (3¾in).

2 Cut out the lining fabric circle and position (wrong side down) in the centre of the puff fabric (wrong side up).

3 Hand sew around the edge of the lining using medium running stitch (the stitching will not show on the front of the finished puff). If the finished piece will be washed, you must ensure the lining is sewn in very well, particularly if the fabric you have chosen frays easily, and backstitch may be a better choice.

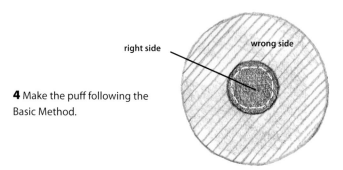

right side · wrong side

4 Make the puff following the Basic Method.

Fusible fabric lining

Fusible fabric lining creates a stiffer finish to your puffs, which can be useful, but it does make it harder to hand sew them onto a background fabric. While the method described is for making a circular contrast centre, simply cut your fabric shapes to match the shape variation of your chosen puffs.

1 Work out the circle size you require (see Tacked [Basted] Lining, step 1). Draw the number of circles you require onto the smooth side of the fusible webbing, and roughly cut out to leave 1–2cm (⅜–¾in) of fusible webbing around each circle.

2 Place the lining fabric on the ironing board wrong side up. Place the drawn-on fusible webbing glue (rough) side down onto the fabric and cover with a Teflon pressing cloth or baking paper. Use a hot iron to press the fusible webbing to the fabric, following the manufacturer's instructions.

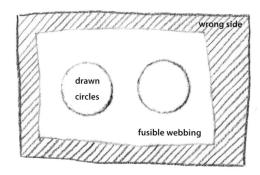

wrong side · drawn circles · fusible webbing

3 When the fabric is cool, cut out the circles to the marked sizes.

4 Prepare the main fabric circles and position on the ironing board with wrong side facing up. Peel the paper backing off the lining circles and place glue side down onto the centre of the main fabric circles. Cover with pressing cloth/paper and press as before. Continue to make the puff following the Basic Method, steps 2–5.

Suffolk puff with contrast centre.

Project Idea:
Suffolk Puff Lampshade

This is made using a vintage lampshade still covered in its original fabric and overlaid with circular Suffolk puffs made in a variety of sizes with contrast centres.

Technique: Suffolk Puffs with Contrast Centre
Material: Pink/orange shot silk dupion and striped silk dupion for the contrast centres

• To work out how many puffs you will require, first make about 10 in different sizes and pin to one section or side of your lampshade. Multiply the number of puffs used by the number of sections on your shade to work out how many puffs you will need in total. As the puffs are different sizes, you may need to make more or less than your estimate, so make sure you have plenty of fabric to start with.

• To make the lampshade, first cover the top and bottom edges of the shade with bias-cut strips of matching silk, and then attach the Suffolk puffs.

• Use small sequin pins to hold the puffs in place. Once you are happy with the arrangement, tack (baste) thoroughly and remove the pins.

• Finally hand-sew the puffs to each other and make a few stitches through into the shade fabric to hold it all together.

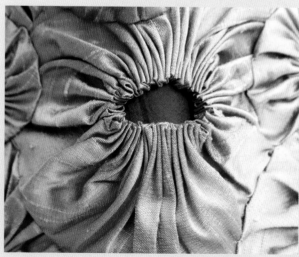

Circle gathering

The techniques here use the basic circle shape to create quite contrasting effects – either gathering a circle shape from the middle of the fabric, or cutting a circle shape out of the fabric. Other shapes could be used but the finished effect would not be radically different.

MATERIAL AND DESIGN NOTES

- Gathering fabrics creates a heavily folded fabric with uneven edges. If the finished work is to be used on a garment, bag or cushion, the gathered piece will need to be stitched to a foundation or base fabric and trimmed to an even size before assembly.

- In many cases, the reverse side of the finished technique may be just as interesting and effective.

- As a general rule, the thicker the fabric, the larger the circles and the stitches used.

Centre hole gather

This technique is basically the reverse of a Suffolk puff; a hole is cut in the middle of a piece of fabric, then sewn up again, to create a decorative starburst gather. The sample shown is made using folded hem and running stitch. A similar effect could be achieved using a hem and cord (see Applied Gathering: Hem Channel), which could be adjustable if both ends of the cord are released.

1 Draw and cut a circle from the fabric, either centrally or offset as required. (To cut the circle out, pinch the fabric with your fingers and make a small snip within the circle line and then use small scissors to cut along the marked line.)

2 Working on the reverse side of the main fabric, fold a small hem over to the back and work running stitch around the circle, and continue following Suffolk Puffs: Basic Method, steps 2–5.

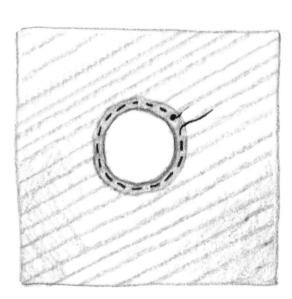

Centre hole gather: the size of the finished starburst gather will be determined by the size of the hole cut, the thickness of the fabric, and the size of stitching used.

Circle edge gathers

The Centre Hole Gather technique can be worked on a section of a circle on fabric edges. In the sample shown, two layers of hemmed fabric are used, but you could work on a raw edge too (see Apply & Layer: Scalloped Edge). Other shapes could also be used for different effects.

1 Layer two fabrics right sides together. Draw part-circles along the edge of the fabric. Sew along the edge and around the part-circles a 5mm (¼in) seam allowance.

2 Cut out the part circles, leaving a 5mm (¼in) seam allowance.

3 Turn the fabric through the right way and turn out the corners; press flat. Work running stitch around the curved edges to create gathers and fasten firmly (see Suffolk Puffs: Basic Method).

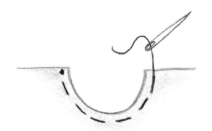

The cut, turned and pressed cut out circle edge before stitching.

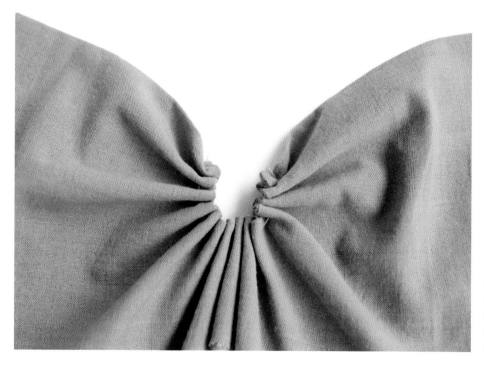

Circle edge gathers showing neat, deep folds created by careful stitching. This technique could be used on a long scarf or on a hem, as well as in layers for decorative work.

Inset puff

This variation on a Suffolk puff is inset into a piece of fabric to create a fabric bulge. It is based on an early 19th century dress made from fine white cotton with puffs in rows around the hem.

1 Cut a circle of fabric and sew running stitches around the edge (see Suffolk Puffs: Basic Method, step 2). A hem can be used if desired but is not necessary. Pull up partially and leave the needle attached.

2 Slash a hole in the base fabric the same size as the radius of the pulled up circle. Gather and flatten the puff so it is the same width across the gathers as the slashed hole.

3 Working from the front of the fabric, push the puff through the slashed hole and pin one end in place. Adjust the gathers until the puff is exactly the same size as the hole then fasten off the thread.

4 Now working from the back, pin the puff in place all the way around using the pins vertically. Sew around the hole and through the puff using small backstitch. Remove the gathering thread if required.

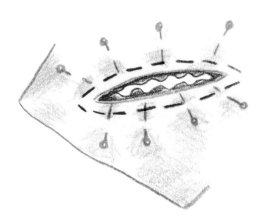

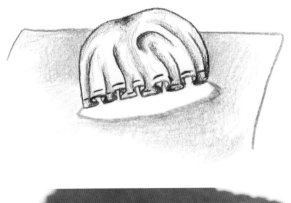

Inset puff, front.

Inset puff, reverse.

Bobbles

When filled with stuffing, these bobbles look like Shibori, the Japanese tie-dyeing technique. When left unstuffed, the effect is more like smocking. Many variations are possible depending on fabric choice, circle size and amount of stuffing used. Bobbles can be placed randomly and made to different sizes, and you could try combining stuffed and unstuffed bobbles in the same piece.

Unstuffed bobbles

In this basic version, the bobbles are tiny. Either side of the fabric can be considered the top, depending on which way you push the fullness of the fabric when you pull up the gathers.

1 Draw the arrangement of the bobble design on the reverse of the fabric. Here a simple off-set grid has been drawn with circles no more than 1cm (⅜in) in diameter but any size can be used.

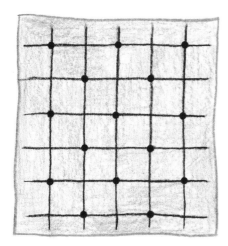

2 With a knotted thread, stitch the circle line using tiny running stitches to end up back where you started; leave the needle attached.

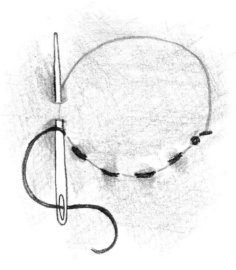

3 Pull up the thread to create gathers. Push the excess fabric to the front or the back depending on the effect desired (the sample shows the excess fabric pushed to the front). Pull up tightly and fasten the thread with two tiny stitches.

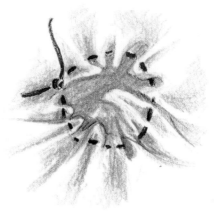

Unstuffed bobbles.

Stuffed bobbles

In this version, small amounts of stuffing are introduced to the circle when the thread is drawn up to create a cavity. Wool stuffing can be used when the finished work will not be heavily used and washing is not required. Polyester stuffing can also be used but it is harder to form into a small ball, so wool is preferred. Hard stuffing, such as polystyrene balls, wooden or plastic beads, can also be used for a different effect and this technique is used to create the Bobble Cushion.

1 Prepare the fabric marking out the design arrangement on the reverse of the fabric (see Unstuffed Bobbles, step 1), using larger circles to allow for filling with stuffing. In this sample the circles are 4cm (1½in) in diameter.

2 Stitch as Unstuffed Bobbles, step 2, then gently pull up the thread to create a cavity. Take a small amount of stuffing and work into a small ball about the size of the cavity. Push the ball in the cavity and pull up the thread.

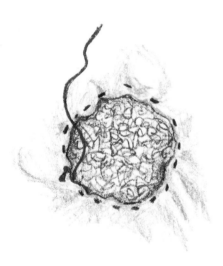

3 Fasten the stitching off close to where you started, using three small stitches hidden in the fold.

Stuffed bobbles worked on velvet fabric: the bobbles are positioned irregularly and close together.

Stuffed bobbles worked on silk fabric: the bobbles are arranged in an offset grid pattern.

Project Idea:
Bobble Cushion

Stuffed bobbles come out beautifully in silk/ viscose velvet, and are incredibly tactile, creating a cushion that can't be put down.

Technique: Stuffed Bobbles
Material: Front fabric – silk/viscose velvet; Interlining – calico; Backing fabric for cushion – organic cotton or quilting cotton

• Cut a piece of front fabric twice the required finished size. For this cushion, which measures 30 x 30cm (12 x 12in), a piece of fabric measuring 60 x 60cm (24 x 24in) was used.

• Work the Stuffed Bobbles technique using 3cm (1⅛in) circles and stuff with polyester stuffing for durability, or wool if preferred.

• Cut an interlining fabric from calico or plain cotton, 5cm (2in) bigger all round than the finished cushion size (35 x 35cm/14 x 14in). Place the interlining fabric right side up and position the bobble velvet fabric on top, right side up. Match the edges and corners together where possible and begin pinning in place.

• Arrange the excess fabric along the edges, folding and tucking the puckered fabric so it matches the interlining fabric. While there may well be excess fabric overlapping the edges in some places, in other places you may have to gently stretch the velvet fabric. Pin in place as you go. Ensure the finished piece is square and not pulling the interlining. It should measure 35cm (14in) square.

• When all the fabric is distributed evenly and pinned in place, tack (baste) by hand using small stitches to keep all the tucks in place, then remove the pins. Trim any excess front fabric away.

• Make the interlined panel into a cushion using your preferred method.

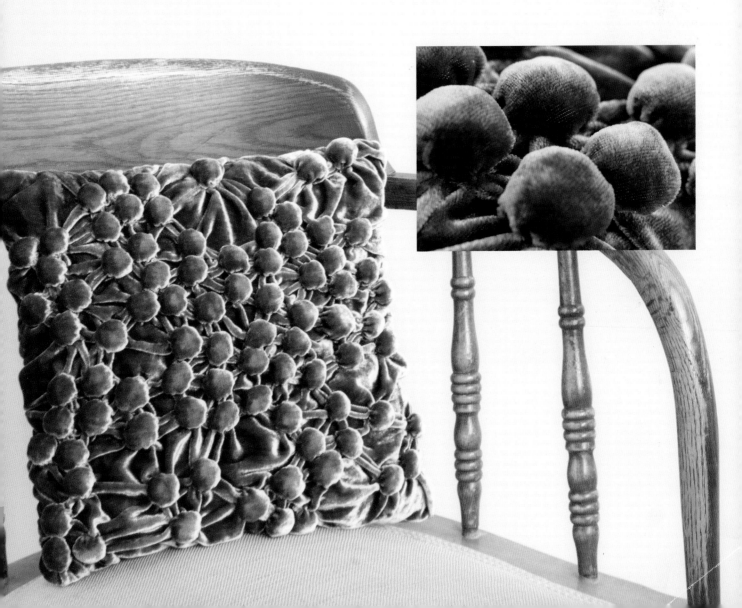

Direct smocking

This technique is usually worked on gingham, as the coloured squares show up the puckers and folds particularly well. However, it could also be worked on spotty fabric but only if the spots are regular. It could be worked on plain fabric but you will need to mark dots on first, and the end result will look more like American Smocking.

MATERIAL AND DESIGN NOTES

- Direct smocking works best on pure cotton gingham; polycotton will not take the fold so well. Vintage gingham is the perfect fabric, if you can get it.

- The gingham fabric provides a ready-made grid for working the stitches and the shading of the boxes creates additional effects.

- Traditionally this technique is combined with embroidery.

Basic method
Follow the Direct Smocking stitch diagram carefully for the order of working the stitching.

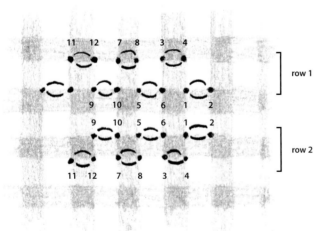

Direct smocking stitch diagram: loops show where the stitch is pulled up.

1 Knot the thread behind the work and bring the needle out at point 1 on the first row. Go back over to point 2 and pick up a couple of threads on that mark. Pull tight.

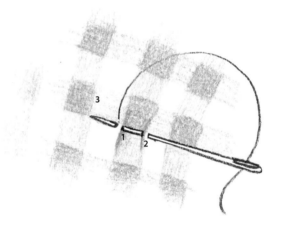

2 Put the needle back in at point 1 then bring it up at point 3 (one square to the top left diagonally).

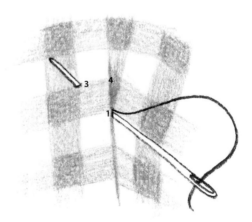

3 Bring the needle over to point 4, pick up a couple of threads, pull tight and put the needle back in at point 3.

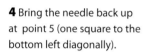

4 Bring the needle back up at point 5 (one square to the bottom left diagonally).

5 Continue to follow the order of stitching across the fabric to complete the first row.

6 Work the second row in the opposite direction, so the first diagonal stitch is made downwards rather than upwards.

Variations

A different effect can be achieved by making the diagonal stitches on the front of the fabric so the thread is prominent; use embroidery thread for the best effect.

You can also vary the technique by bringing the thread out on the surface between stitches, rather than behind.

Direct smocking: basic method.

American Smocking

American smocking is worked entirely on the reverse of the fabric and creates a dense puckered design on the front of the fabric. Traditionally the design is marked out as a series of dots, but a grid is much more effective.

MATERIAL AND DESIGN NOTES

- Almost any weight of fabric can be used, but fine fabrics may collapse too easily; this can be remedied by using plain or grid iron-on interfacing to stiffen the fabric.

- Thick fabrics should be stitched using a large, widely-spaced grid, while finer fabrics can be smocked on a smaller grid pattern (5mm/¼in).

- If you mark out your design with a vanishing pen or tailor's chalk, the stitched side of the design could be used as the front.

- There are many more designs possible than it is possible to show here, and you could easily create your own variations.

Prepare the fabric

The grid can be transferred to the reverse of the fabric using any of the marking methods, including iron-on transfer, vanishing pen or tailor's chalk. You may find it helpful to transfer the markings from the chart as well as the grid. *Note:* Loops show where the stitch is pulled up and solid arrowed lines show where the stitch is left loose.

While the fastest way of preparing the design onto the back of the fabric is iron-on grid interfacing, you will find that it is harder to stitch through. The interfacing will stiffen the fabric, making it hold the shape well and the folds will be much crisper and more defined. However, a softer finish may be preferable and experimentation is the key.

Grid interfacing is most commonly available in 2.5cm (1in) squares and this has been used for all the samples shown. While 1cm (⅜in) grid interfacing is also available this square size is probably too small except for the finest of fabrics, so lines at 2cm (¾in) would have to be drawn over the interfacing.

If using grid interfacing, draw the design directly onto it. If using a hand-drawn or transferred grid, mark the row numbers on the fabric for ease of reference.

Basic method

1 Prepare your fabric and transfer your chosen design onto the reverse of the fabric. Thread your needle with a strong thread, such as polyester, ensuring it is long enough to complete one row of the design and that it matches your fabric; make a knot at the end of the thread.

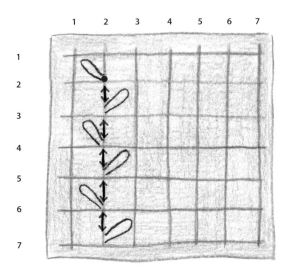

2 You are ready to begin stitching. Each stitch picks up only a couple of threads, which hardly show from the front. Make the first stitch at the start point shown on the diagram, making two tiny stitches to fasten.

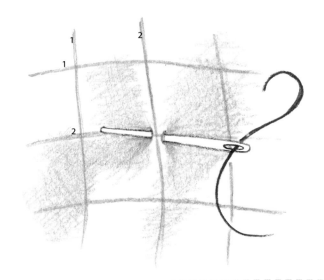

3 Take the needle diagonally to the next point and pull up.

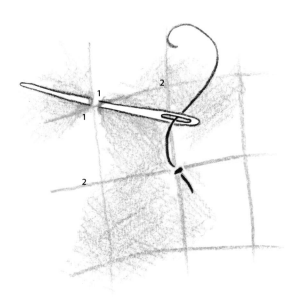

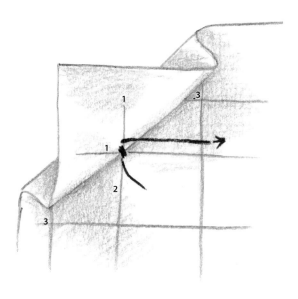

4 Knot the thread by going back through the stitch.

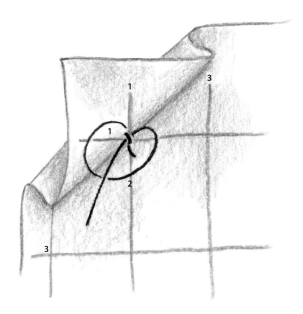

5 Make the next stitch, which is an unpulled stitch. Pick up threads at the required point then knot the stitch as in step 4, so that this stitch does not pull when you pull up the following stitch. Continue following the diagram to the end of the row. Return to the top to start the second row, using a new piece of thread.

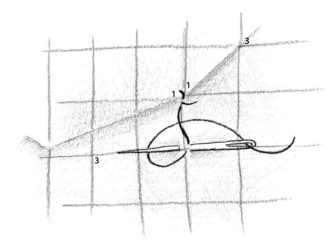

Lattice

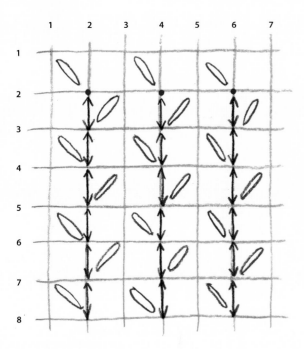

Lattice stitch diagram.

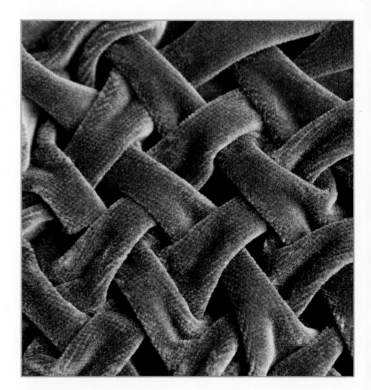

Lattice design worked in velvet.

Note: On the stitch diagrams, loops show where the stitch is pulled up and arrowed lines show where the stitch is left loose.

Lattice design worked in tafetta.

Arrows

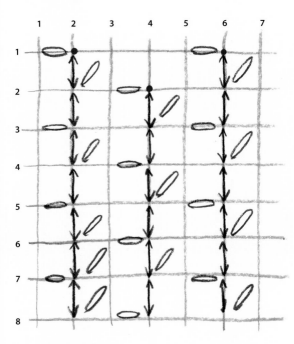

Arrows stitch diagram.

Arrows design in fine wool suiting, front.

Arrows design in fine wool suiting, reverse.

Grid

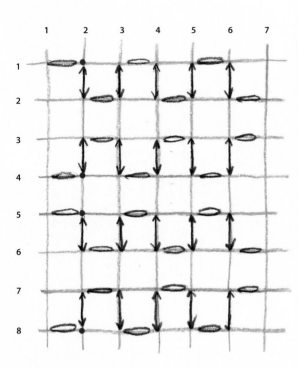

Grid stitch diagram.

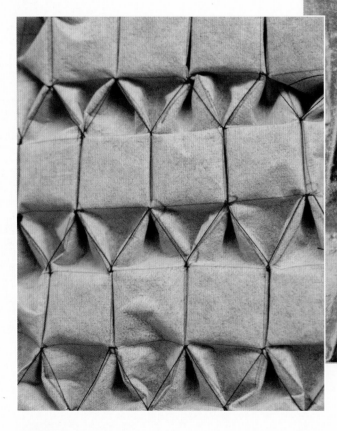

Grid design in silk dupion: front
and reverse.

Boxes

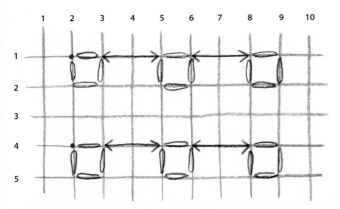

Boxes stitch diagram: the samples that follow are created using the same stitching guidelines shown here with variations in the manipulation of the fabric made after sewing.

Boxes design in organic cotton: the folds are pushed to the back of the work and the corner puffs emphasized.

Pressed boxes design in silk dupion: the folds are left to the front and then pressed down in neat arrangements.

Close boxes

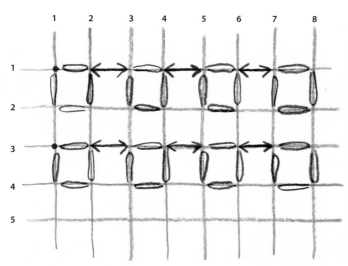

Close boxes stitch diagram: loops show where the stitch is pulled up and arrowed lines show where the stitch is left loose. In this variation of Boxes each square is worked. Working on the reverse of the fabric, stitch around the box as marked, picking up a couple of threads at each corner, then pull up all the stitches together. Fasten firmly, then make one unpulled stitch to start the next box. Continue working across in this manner.

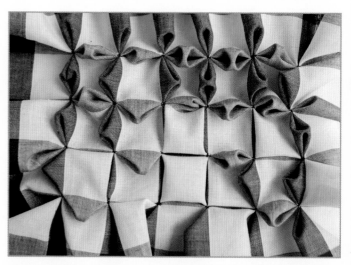

Flowers worked on a soft, polycotton gingham which drapes well. It uses the same technique as Unpressed Close Boxes but worked in a different way. It is particularly effective in gingham (2.5cm/1in squares) due to the shading, but it can be worked also on plain fabric if a grid is drawn on in vanishing pen before stitching. To work, stitch the design from the front, pulling up the threads tightly then moving to the next box on the reverse of the fabric. Push the folds to the front to create the flower effect. The lower part of the sample shows how the technique works if you do not push all the folds to the front.

Unpressed close boxes in cotton voile: the folds have been left to the front and unpressed, while the side folds have been finger pressed and manipulated into shape. The piece is worked with iron-on interfacing, which creates some stiffness in the fabric to allow for manipulation.

Reverse of flowers: this shows the dark green blobs where the folds have been pushed through to the front. This is also an effective texture and could be used as the front fabric.

English smocking

Traditional English smocking, as seen in farming smocks, is created with a series of fine gathers over which embroidery stitches are worked, before the preparatory gathering stitches are removed.

MATERIAL AND DESIGN NOTES

- There are many different stitches that can be used for English Smocking such as cable, herringbone and trellis, but the basic preparatory technique is the same.

- An evenly woven fabric such as linen or cotton is easiest to use. It will hold the gathers nicely, and it should be worked on the straight grain only.

- The embroidery thread used should be a high-twist cotton or linen, such as perle; stranded cotton (floss) may get too fluffy and snap.

1 Use a new thread for each row of stitching and knot firmly at the start. Go in at the first dot and out at the next, creating even running stitch across the fabric. Repeat on all the rows.

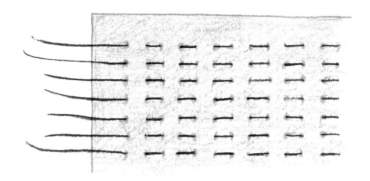

Prepare the fabric
Unless you are working on a squared fabric, such as gingham, you will need to make the markings for the gathering stitches on the reverse of the fabric, with each dot 5mm (¼in) apart and each row 5mm (¼in) apart. This can be done in several ways.
Method 1: Use a ruler and marking pen or pencil to mark rows of dots,
Method 2: Use smocking dot iron-on transfers if available.
Method 3: Use a template made in fine plastic or light card with holes punched in.
Method 4: Use squared paper, punched through to make pencil marks onto the fabric.

2 Pull up the threads gently and slide the gathers along the fabric, gathering up quite tightly, but not so much that you can't get the needle in to make the stitches.

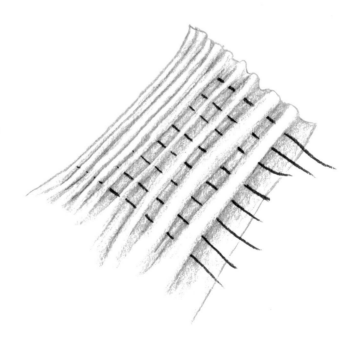

Basic method
For the sample Spot Honeycomb has been used. This is one of the most contemporary-looking and relatively simple variations and it creates a nice stretchy fabric. The size and depth of the folds will depend on the size of the gathering you create to start with and this sample is worked with 5mm (¼in) spacing. The gathering and smocking takes up about two-thirds of the fabric.

3 When all the threads are pulled up evenly, wrap loose thread around holding pins or sew in the gathering threads and trim the excess. These hold the gathers firm until you have completed the smocking stitches (they will be removed later). Steam the piece to help set the gathers.

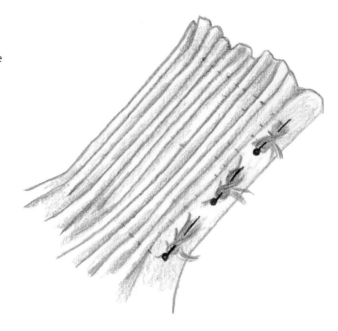

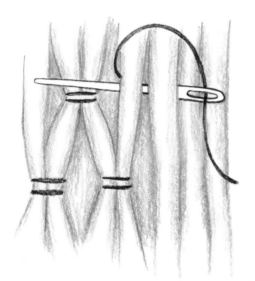

4 Spot honeycomb smocking is worked from the top left, and two rows are worked at the same time. Work two small backstitches over the first pair of tubes, catching them together just near the surface and pulling them firmly.

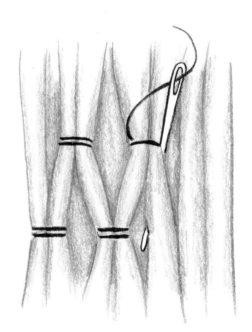

5 Push the needle diagonally down the second tube to come out on the line of the gathering stitches. Make another pair of backstitches to hold those tubes together. Then push the needle back up the right-hand tube to the next pair of tubes and continue to the end of the row.

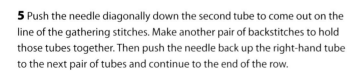

6 For the second row, you may find it easier to turn the work upside down and work left to right again, rather than right to left.

7 Continue until the whole piece is smocked, then carefully unpick the gathering threads to allow the smocking to expand.

Note: A hand-crank machine called a Princess Pleater can also be used to pre-gather and stitch fabric – it contains many needles which automatically make the stitching for you, but takes a long time to set up and only works with fine fabrics. This type of machine is hard to acquire *and* it is expensive.

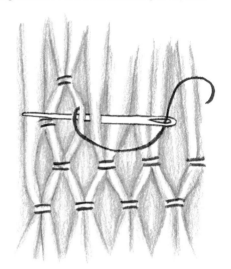

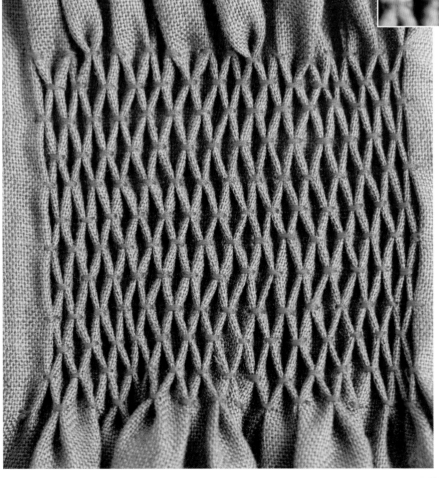

Spot honeycomb smocking: approx 30cm (12in) of fabric was gathered to produce about 10cm (4in) of smocking.

Apply & Layer

Stitch and slash

A sandwich of fabrics is stitched together along the bias, then the upper layers are cut to reveal the layers beneath. The resulting rows can be manipulated to create various effects, and the variations are seemingly endless depending on the number of fabric layers included, the colours chosen, and the folding and stitching techniques used.

MATERIAL AND DESIGN NOTES

- Choose a firm fabric such as cotton for the bottom layer, and ensure that the upper layers of fabric are cut on the straight grain.

- Tools are available to enable long rows of slashing to be done easily on firm fabrics (see Tool Guide).

- When working with three or more fabric layers, and particularly thick fabrics, an even-feed machine foot can be very useful.

- To create a fluffy surface known as faux chenille, work in layers of quilting-weight cottons and stitch in close rows, then wash and fluff up.

Basic method

1 Cut the layers of fabric to the same size ensuring that the grain is straight. (A minimum of three layers is most effective.)

2 Mark diagonal lines on the top or bottom fabric layer (either is fine – use the bottom fabric if the top layer is hard to mark). The distance between the stitching lines will vary depending on the thickness of the fabric sandwich, but approx 1cm (⅜in) is a good starting point for three to five layers. Experiment with different spacing, but remember you will need to be able to get the scissors into the channel to cut it open. Tack (baste) together the layers of fabric, right side up.

3 Sew the marked lines using a medium stitch length. Starting with the middle line, sew one row of stitching on either side of it. Working outwards, turn the work each time to sew in the opposite direction on each marked line.

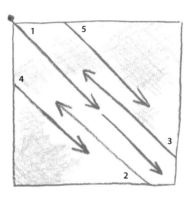

4 Working from the edge of the fabric, insert the scissors between the bottom and upper layers and cut along. Take care to keep the slash centred between the stitching and aim to make a clean line. When cutting the layers, always check you don't cut the bottom layer.

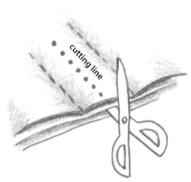

The top layer of fabric is a finely striped silk dupion, with the stripes acting as a contrast to the bias-cut slashes. The middle layer is red cotton with pink bottom layer.

Exploring variations

Cross stitching

The slashes can be manipulated and sewn down by hand, by machine, or simply pressed and steamed. In this sample the folds are sewn down with a line of machine stitching worked across the folds.

Place the work on the sewing machine so that you are working diagonally across the stitched and slashed lines. Fold back the first flap and sew over. Continue to fold and stitch over each slash, making sure you keep a straight line as you go (if you prefer, you can mark a line in tailor's chalk first).

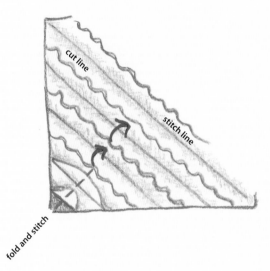

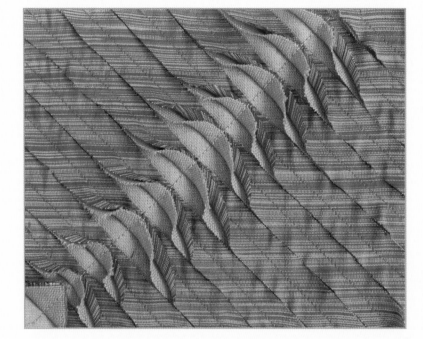

Cross stitching allows the middle and bottom layer to show where folded back so choose fabrics that give good contrast for effective results.

Multi-layering of fabrics

Different fabrics create a variety of textures and effects. In this sample, eight fabrics including felt, fleece, chiffon, net and corduroy have been used. When working with thick fabrics, use a longer stitch length (4mm or above) and an even-feed machine foot to avoid the fabric bunching up. Sew the stitching lines 1.5–2cm (⅝–¾in) apart depending on the thickness of the fabric sandwich.

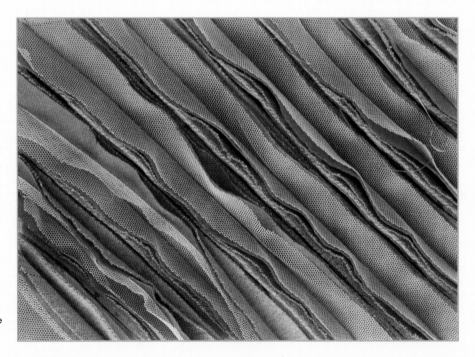

Multiple layers of fabric puff up to create a dense texture.

Working on the straight grain

Although most-often worked on the bias, the slash and stitch
technique can also be worked on the straight grain of the
fabric, as seen in the samples below.

The fabric is cut and stitched along the straight grain, with widely
spaced stitching rows. The edges have been allowed to fray.

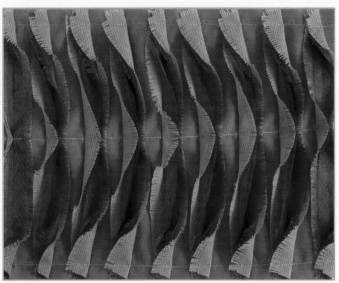

The slashes are folded and stitched in one direction on the upper edge
and in the opposite direction on the lower edge, to create a wave effect.
(This variation is also very effective on bias-cut stitch and slash.)

Fold and stitch variations

These samples are all created using the same base: a sandwich of five fabric layers – cotton, needlecord,
chiffon, silk, cotton – stitched in rows 1.5cm (⅝in) apart.

Variation 1

Referring to Cross Stitching, fold over and sew down one row. Now fold and sew
another row in the opposite direction. Between the two folded and stitched lines,
bring the fabric together on either side and sew over the top edges to hold in place.

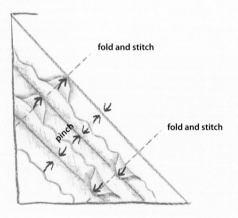

Variation 2

Bring the cut edges over to the centre cut line, folding flat. Use a cross-shaped stitch to hold the flaps flat. Alternate the folds, leaving one line unfolded in between.

Variation 3

In this sample the second layer of fabric – the needlecord – is cut but left unfolded. Fold the edges over to the cut line and stitch flat with single long stitches. Bring the next edge over to the same place. Repeat, alternating folds on the next row.

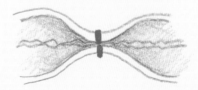

Quilting

A quilt is, very simply, two or more fabric layers stitched together, either by hand or by machine. Normally a quilt has a layer of thick wadding (batting) sandwiched in between a top and lining fabric. In a traditional quilt, the backing or lining fabric will show on the back of the piece, although quilted pieces can be made where the back does not show.

MATERIAL AND DESIGN NOTES

- Both fabric and wadding (batting) may shrink after washing; some prefer to work with pre-washed fabrics, while others favour the puckered effect after washing a quilted piece.

- When making a quilted piece where the backing will not be seen it is just as important to take shrinkage into account as when making a traditional quilt where the backing will be seen.

- When quilting large pieces, use a quilting thread that has a high twist, as it is less likely to break.

Prepare the fabric

Whether working hand or machine quilting, the preparation of the fabric is the same.

1 Transfer the quilting design to the right side of the top fabric.

2 Make the quilt sandwich as follows: place the lining fabric right side down (if the back is visible in the finished project); place the wadding (batting) on top of the lining fabric; and finally, lay the top fabric face up. Pin together with long, straight pins or safety pins.

3 Using long threads, tack (baste) the layers together, starting with the outside edges, then through the centre in a cross. For large pieces, tack (baste) lines about 15cm (6in) apart. Remove the pins before quilting by hand or machine.

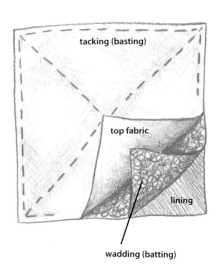

The overall size of the quilt or quilted piece may shrink slightly due to the quilting. Cut the wadding (batting) and backing fabric slightly bigger than the top fabric if required.

Hand quilting

Hand quilting is time-consuming but worthwhile as it creates a very different effect to machine quilting. Hand stitches can be made in a variety of threads including embroidery cotton, silk, hand-dyed varigated threads and even non-standard thread like dental floss.

1 Start the quilting using a thread about 40cm (16in) long. Fasten the thread at the edge of the work.

2 Sew the design with a 2–3mm (⅛in) long running stitch, going vertically through from top to bottom.

The stitches you use for hand quilting can be tiny and precise, or you can make them large and bold so that the stitching is the main feature. You can also quilt using embroidery stitches such as chain stitch.

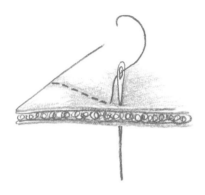

3 To finish work a tiny backstitch over the last quilting stitch on the front or back as preferred.

Machine quilted cotton with thin bamboo wadding creates a fine, thin quilt. Polyester wadding is useful if a thicker effect is required.

Machine quilting

Machine quilting is much faster than hand quilting, but it creates a flatter and more solid finish. An even-feed foot is recommended for sewing through several layers, and is essential for a thick quilted fabric. Practise on a quilt made from offcuts to adjust the tension correctly. If quilting in evenly spaced lines, use a quilting guide – a small metal bar which attaches to your machine foot – to keep the distance between the rows.

1 Turn the flywheel and put the needle up and down a couple of times. Pull on the thread to bring the bobbin thread to the surface. Hold both the threads when you start sewing to avoid tangles. Fasten the thread by sewing a few stitches at 0.5mm long.

2 To start, increase the stitch length to about 3–4mm or the desired size, and sew along the quilting design, moving the quilt around to follow the design. For large pieces, quilt from the centre outwards.

3 End the stitching in the same way as you started, by reducing the stitch length, pulling up the bobbin thread and cutting off each thread as you go.

The density of quilting will affect the look of the finished quilt. Lots of stitching will produce a flat and stiff quilted fabric, while widely spaced lines help to retain the puffiness or loft of the wadding (batting). However, the thickness of the finished quilt will also depend on the loft of wadding (batting) used.

 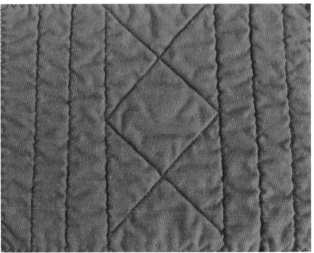

Washing a quilted piece will alter its texture. The wadding (batting) and the fabrics may shrink to different degrees to create a puckered, worn effect. In this sample both the top (red) cotton fabric and the bamboo wadding (batting) have shrunk, but the (pink) polycotton lining fabric has not.

Hand-tied quilting

In hand-tied quilting, knots, rather than lines of stitching, hold the fabric layers together. Embroidery thread is ideal for hand-tied quilts.

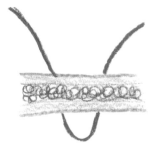
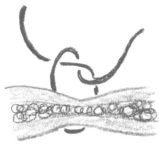

1 Prepare the quilt sandwich as Basic Method: Prepare the Fabric, step 2.

2 Thread a length of embroidery thread on a long, sharp needle, such as a crewel needle. Working from the top, go through all the layers and come back up about 3–6mm (⅛–¼in) away, leaving a tail about 10cm (4in) long.

3 Tie the ends of the thread together and cut the tails to about 1cm (⅜in) long.

4 Repeat at intervals no more than 10cm (4in) apart.

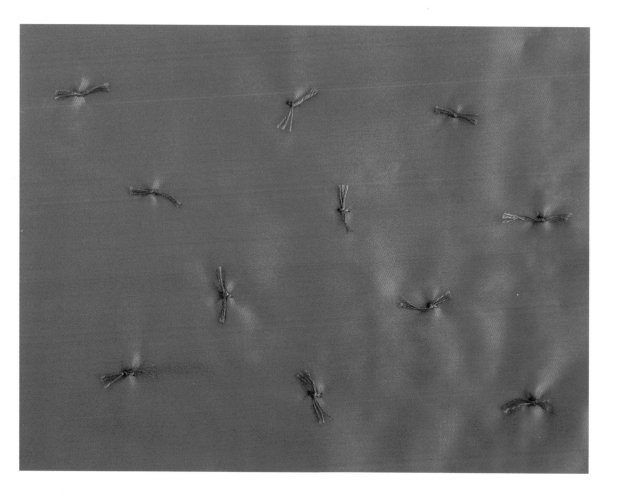

Cut surface quilting

This is a combination of Quilting and Stitch and Slash techniques, where the top layer of fabric and the wadding (batting) are cut close up to the stitching so the layers pop up. The Basic Method, described using a felt fabric, requires just minor changes when working with different materials as described in the variations.

MATERIAL AND DESIGN NOTES

- A wadding (batting) layer or layers is sandwiched in between a top and base layer to create a quilt sandwich.
- The effects of using different waddings (battings) can be seen in the variations described.
- Use a sturdy fabric for the base layer, such as medium-weight cotton or calico.
- The design motif used needs to be a solid shape.

2 Use an even-feed foot and small stitches (2mm) to sew the design, reducing the stitch length to 0.5mm at the start and end to fasten. Pull the threads to the back, knot and cut off.

3 Use sharp, fine-pointed scissors to make a tiny snip 2mm (³⁄₃₂in) from the inside of the stitched line, cutting along the inside edge of the stitching. Cut through the layers of wadding (batting) but do not cut the backing fabric.

Basic method

1 Cut the wadding (batting), top fabric layer and backing fabric to the same size. Draw the design onto the top layer, if required, before layering the quilt sandwich. Place the backing fabric face up, the wadding (batting) in the middle and the felt on top, right side up. Pin and baste (see Quilting: Basic Method: Prepare the Fabric, step 3).

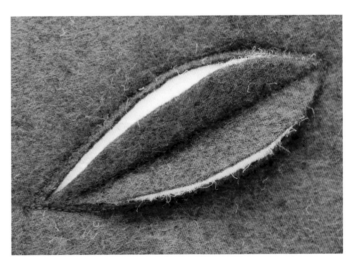

Material variations

Fabric

Work as Basic Method but first back the fabric with an iron-on interfacing of an appropriate weight, working on the reverse side, to stop the cut edge from fraying excessively.

Leather

Choose a fine leather (or suede) material. Work as Basic Method but use a sharp craft knife to cut the fabric, applying gentle pressure so you don't cut through the backing. Use fine-pointed scissors to cut the wadding (batting) if necessary. *Note:* The sample shown uses two layers of wool felt as an alternative wadding (batting).

Wadding (batting) variations

Types of wadding (batting)

Green wadding (batting) is made from recycled plastic bottles. Polyester wadding (batting) can also be dyed using commercial dyes designed for synthetic fabrics. Bamboo, wool, cotton and other natural waddings (battings) are also available but, as these tend to shed fibres, they may not produce the clean edge of the synthetic wadding (batting). Different effects can also be achieved by using several layers of your chosen wadding (batting).

Five layers of different fabric, both thick and thin, have been used here to create a dense, colourful multi-layered wadding (batting)..

Two layers of fleece fabric have been used as a wadding (batting).

Wadding (batting) fold back

In this sample, the backing fabric chosen is in a contrasting colour to the top fabric; the top and wadding (batting) layers are folded back and stitched into position to reveal it.

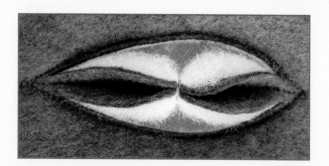

Trapunto

Trapunto quilting uses stuffing to create a design from padded areas between two layers of fabric. A top and a backing fabric layer are stitched together; the backing layer is then cut open and the stuffing added between the two fabric layers. The design can be worked with running stitch, backstitch or machine stitch, and stretch and transparent fabrics can be used; however the Basic Method described below is the simplest.

MATERIAL AND DESIGN NOTES

- Traditionally merino wool tops are used to stuff fine or detailed shapes, but these cannot be washed. Washable polyester stuffing can be used instead, but this is harder to stuff into small areas for detailed designs.
- Small, detailed designs are very hard to stuff effectively and beginners should use bold, simple shapes with the minimum of narrow lines, points and complex detail.
- Trapunto works best on plain fabric with a slight sheen (it barely shows on a patterned fabric). Use a tight-weave backing fabric, such as cotton sheeting or other plain-woven fabric, in a similar weight to the top fabric.
- If working on lightweight or transparent fabrics, use silk organza as the backing fabric.
- Where the reverse of trapunto might be exposed, such as in a garment, it should always be lined.

2 Draw a simple, bold design onto the backing fabric with chalk, vanishing pen or other suitable marker (pencil will show on light colours, so only use this method if the top fabric and thread used are dark).

3 Take a contrasting embroidery thread and fasten the thread in the backing fabric, just outside the stitching line. Work running stitch around the outline, taking care to keep the stitches even on the top fabric.

Basic method

1 Put the top fabric right side down; place the backing fabric on top, right side up. Pin then tack (baste) the piece around the edges and diagonally across the centre.

4 When all the outline stitching is complete, remove the tacking (basting); press the top fabric to remove any creases and to set the stitches into the fabric.

5 Each motif is stuffed individually. To create the cut in the backing fabric, separate the top and back layers by pinching the fabrics between finger and thumb. Holding the backing fabric only, make a tiny snip in the fabric and cut to enlarge slightly, cutting along the bias grain of the fabric where possible.

6 Push small amounts of stuffing into the cavity. Use tweezers, scissor points or a knitting needle to poke the stuffing into place. Stuff the edges of the shape first, and then fill the centre (do not overstuff as this will cause the fabric to pucker around the stitching).

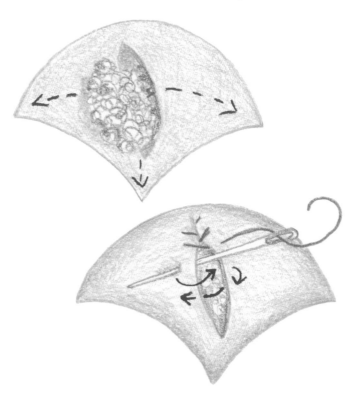

7 Sew up the slit by stitching from inside to outside without pulling too hard, again to avoid puckering the fabric.

This design is based on a traditional shell patchwork shape. Trapunto is effective when worked on either individual shapes or all-over quilting. In an all-over design, some areas could be stuffed and some left unstuffed to create a different texture, but consistency is vital; if stuffing the whole design, do try to keep the level of stuffing the same in all of the shapes to avoid puckering the fabric.

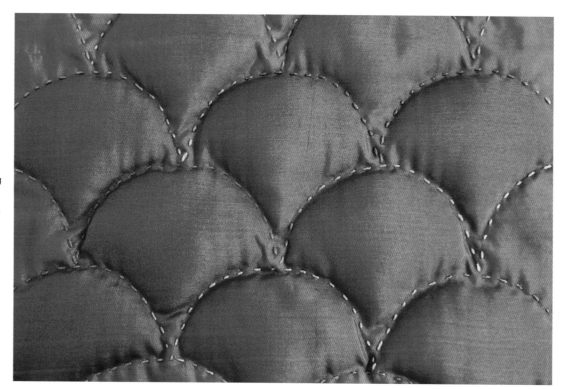

Stitching and fabric variations

Backstitch

For very detailed shapes, a solid line of stitching is required to produce a firm line to show the shape effectively. This can be done by machine or by hand using backstitch.

When working with backstitch, the stitching must be worked on the top fabric, *not* the backing fabric. Use a vanishing pen or other marker to draw the design, then prepare the fabric layers as Basic Method, step 1. Fasten the thread on the back then work around the shape in backstitch. Slash and stuff as the Basic Method, using very tiny pieces of stuffing to fill any awkward shapes.

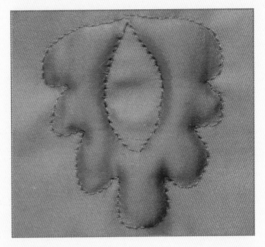

Backstitch: this sample is worked on lightweight silk satin.

Appliqué combination

Trapunto can be combined with simple appliqué. To apply the fabric shapes to the main fabric, use stitching around the edge rather than a heat-fix fabric (see Appliqué). The main fabric behind the appliquéd motif is then slashed open and stuffed as the Basic Method.

Appliqué combination: a piece of felt has been applied to the main fabric using invisible stitching.

Machine-stitched

A firm line of stitching can also be achieved by using the sewing machine to create the outline. Prepare the fabric layers (see Basic Method) with the design on the backing fabric or the top fabric as you prefer. Use a short stitch length and carefully manipulate the fabric whilst stitching to create the correct shape. Continue as the Basic Method.

Medium-weight cotton works well in trapunto with machine stitching.

Jersey

Unlike woven fabrics, jersey trapunto can be heavily stuffed to create a dense surface design on either lightweight cotton jersey or heavier knitted fabrics. Work as normal but stuff the shapes solidly, checking on progress and adjusting until the motif is raised but not puckering.

Cotton t-shirt jersey using tiny hand running stitches.

Wool/heavy fabrics

When trapunto is worked on a heavyweight, thick fabric, it requires dense stuffing and simple, bold shapes.

This thick wool felt is stitched with cotton thread in running stitch and heavily stuffed with wool.

Velvet

It is possible to work trapunto on velvet. The same running stitch motif has been worked here with very different effects. To the left, the design is stitched with doubled polyester sewing thread, which is almost invisible. To the right, the design is stitched with two strands of stranded embroidery thread (floss) to create a bolder line and a more obvious motif.

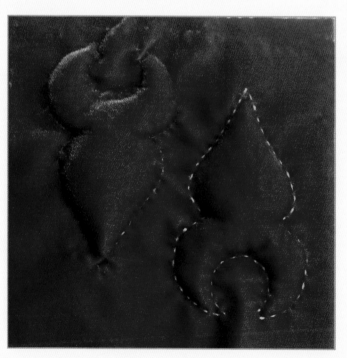

Transparent fabric

Interesting effects can be produced using transparent top fabric combined with coloured stuffing. This sample uses silk organza for the top fabric and plain white cotton as the backing fabric. Coloured merino wool is used for the stuffing. Work as Basic Method and stuff carefully as lumps will be very obvious.

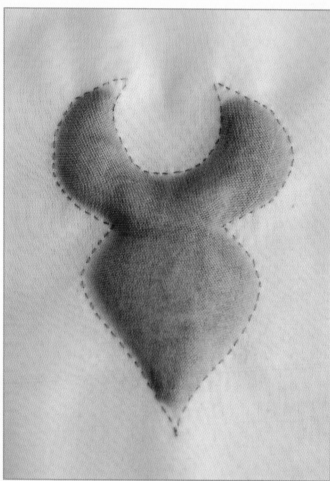

Trapunto worked on transparent fabric is also known as Shadow Quilting, and could also be worked by machine stitching or using backstitch.

Trapunto worked on velvet with running stitch. The left-hand sample is stitched with doubled polyester sewing thread, which is almost invisible. The right-hand sample is stitched with two strands of stranded cotton (floss), which creates a bolder line and a more obvious motif.

Corded trapunto

This technique is very similar to Trapunto quilting, but the design is worked in narrow, parallel lines and the channels created are filled with yarn rather than stuffing.

MATERIAL AND DESIGN NOTES

- The design is made up of channels created from two lines of stitching a few millimetres apart.

- In the sample shown the channels are 6mm (¼in) wide and two strands of chunky-weight knitting yarn is used to stuff. Smaller channels and finer yarn could also be used.

- Straight lines and wide curves are best as short channels and tight corners are difficult to stuff. The yarn stuffing has to come out of the fabric at each turn, so lots of turns would create many holes in the backing.

- Use washable yarn if you intend to launder your finished piece or wool yarn if not.

Basic method

1 Prepare the fabric layers as Trapunto, Basic Method, step 1 and transfer the design to the top or backing fabric as you prefer.

2 Stitch the parallel lines of the design by machine, running stitch or backstitch, as required. Press your work when complete.

3 Thread a doubled length of yarn measuring 50–60cm (20–24in) into your needle, matching the yarn ends. Starting in the middle of a straight channel insert the needle through the backing fabric only and along the channel, pulling the yarn through.

4 Push the needle through to the corner or turning point and bring the needle back out of the backing. Cut the exit hole slightly bigger if required. Pull the yarn right through, untangling any knots, so it lies flat in the channel. Pull through until 3cm (1⅛in) remains sticking out of the first hole.

5 To turn the corner, reinsert the needle in the same exit hole and work the yarn up the next channel. You may find it easier to pre-cut the exit holes at corners and tight curves.

6 When the stuffing is complete, cut the ends of the yarn close to the backing fabric and tuck the fluffy ends into the channel.

Stuffed squares

Stuffed squares are sometimes used to create quilts and are known as Baby's Puffs. Each square is basically a small, fat quilt, and finished squares can be easily joined together in rows and patterns. The Basic Method described can be used to make rectangular or any other tessellating shape.

MATERIAL AND DESIGN NOTES

- In the sample shown, the top fabric is 2cm (¾in) larger than the backing fabric. The top fabric can be cut larger to allow more stuffing to be inserted.

- To create flatter puffs, cut the top fabric only 1cm (⅜in) larger than your backing fabric.

- Prepare the stuffing before you start sewing so all the puffs end up the same. Use polyester stuffing for washable pieces.

- Keep the seam allowances accurate to enable the puffs to fit together properly.

Basic method

1 Cut base squares 2cm (¾in) larger than the finished size you require. (In this sample each base square is cut to 8cm [3⅛in].) Cut top squares 2–3cm (¾–1⅛in) larger than the base squares. (In this sample each top square is 10cm [4in].) Press the fabric squares.

2 Take a base and top square; match the first two corners together and pin. Pin the second corners together, creating a pleat in the centre. Fold the pleat towards the second corner so it is easy to sew over.

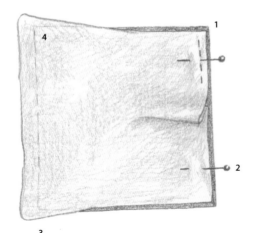

3 Using a 1cm (⅜in) seam allowance, start sewing at corner 1 and sew over the pleat to corner 2.

4 Pivot at corner 2, then line up the top and base fabric so the corners meet and create the pleat. You can pin if required but it is faster to hold the fabric in place as you go. Continue until three sides of the square have been sewn.

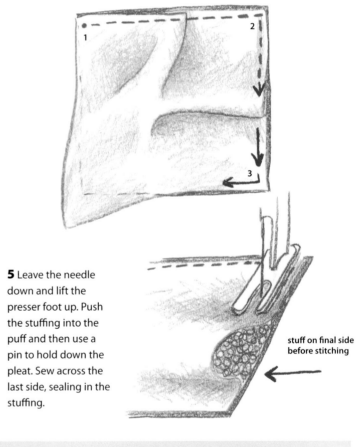

stuff on final side before stitching

5 Leave the needle down and lift the presser foot up. Push the stuffing into the puff and then use a pin to hold down the pleat. Sew across the last side, sealing in the stuffing.

Note: If your prefer, you can prepare and pin the three sides of the square before you start sewing, then remove the puff from the machine to stuff, before returning it to the machine to sew up the last side. This method may work better for particularly slippery fabrics. To make sewing the puffs together less fiddly you can make and sew them together in sections leaving one side open, then stuff a whole row or block at a time.

Joining puffs

Join the puffs together in rows, then in small sections to make a large 'puff' quilt. It is important to ensure that all the puffs are the same size – if your seam allowances have varied then the puffs will vary in size and won't fit together perfectly.

1 Place two puffs facing together and match the corners. Pin in place.

2 Sew with the base fabric facing up and sew along the previous stitching line to prevent the stitching from showing on the front.

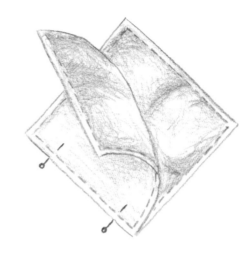

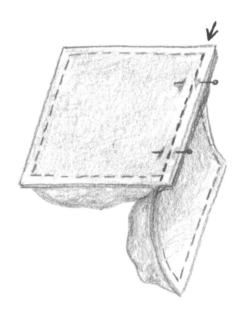

Puffs in patchwork

In this sample, one puff has been used as the centre of a log cabin-style patchwork panel. Follow the diagram to construct the block.

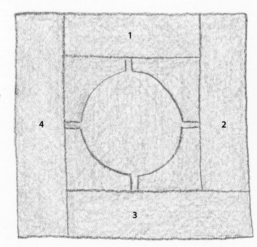

Appliqué

Appliqué covers a wide number of methods for adding pieces of fabric to a background material, usually for decorative purposes. Fabric motifs can be applied with heat-fix fusible webbing and/or stitching, and while machine stitching is quicker, several hand-stitching methods are also described. Appliqué can also be used in combination with other techniques, such as Trapunto for example.

MATERIAL AND DESIGN NOTES

- Fusible webbing appliqué makes the cutting of complicated shapes easy without the fabric fraying or distorting.

- When working fusible webbing appliqué, remember the design will be reversed so take care if using letters or an unsymmetrical design.

- Machine-stitched appliqué is a quick way to add decorative motifs but fabrics may need to be interfaced first to prevent puckering.

- Hand appliqué works best in fabrics that don't fray too much or for fine fabrics such as lawn.

Fusible webbing appliqué

Fusible webbing is fabric glue attached to paper that is activated by the application of heat. The paper is removed in the final stage when the appliqué is heat bonded to the fabric. Sewing down is not required for normal use but decorative stitching can enhance the appliqué. The glue makes the fabric stiffer than normal, so hand stitching through the appliqué may be difficult, and machine stitching will be easier (see Machine-Stitched Appliqué).

Note: The finished appliqué is usually washable, but do check the manufacturer's instructions. Use a Teflon pressing cloth or baking paper to avoid damage to your iron and ironing board.

1 Cut pieces of fusible webbing 1–2cm (⅜–¾in) larger all round than your chosen motif. Place the glue side down onto the wrong side of the fabric (the glue side will feel slightly rough to the touch). Cover with a cloth or paper and iron following the manufacturer's instructions.

2 Reverse the design (if necessary) and trace in pencil directly onto the fusible webbing paper. Cut out with sharp paper scissors.

Fine organic cotton fused onto coarser linen background gives a contrast of textures.

fusible webbing

3 Arrange the motifs on the fabric and when you are happy with the arrangement, peel off the paper backing. If it is hard to remove, crumple the edges of the appliqué slightly, which will release the paper. Ensure the appliqués are correctly positioned, cover with a pressing cloth, and press according to the manufacturer's instructions.

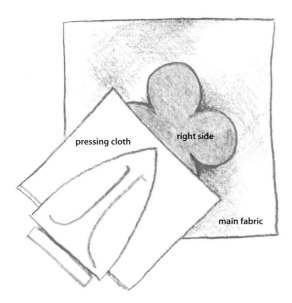

Layered fusible webbing

Trace, cut out and prepare all the motifs. Bond the first motif to the fabric, then build up the layers one at a time.

Contrasting colours work well with layered fusible webbing. Patterned fabrics are also suitable.

Machine-stitched appliqué

Shapes can be stitched by machine using a variety of stitching techniques. First, to stop the fabric puckering, motifs can be fixed down with fusible webbing (see Fusible Webbing Appliqué), or backed with interfacing to stabilize it doesn't stretch or fray while you work.

Apply iron-on interfacing to the wrong side of the appliqué fabric and draw the required shapes. For a neat edge, always interface more than you need and then cut out the shape, so you can be sure that the interfacing goes right to the edge. Cut out the motif and tack (baste) in position on the main fabric. Alternatively, small appliqué pins can be used, but take care when sewing around them.

Machine-stitch the appliqué design in place using one of the following methods.

Faux-blanket stitch

If your machine has faux-blanket stitch (sometimes called overcast stitch), it can be used on motifs that have interfacing on the reverse or that have been stuck down with fusible webbing. Practise the stitch on a scrap of fabric. Position the motif so the straight line of the stitch is on the inside of the motif while the 'legs' go just over the edge of the fabric. Work slowly, rotating the fabric so the stitching stays the correct distance from the edge. Pivot at corners and tight curves.

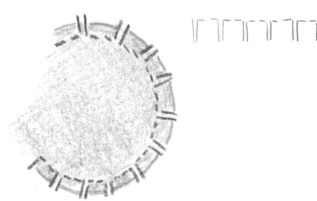

Faux blanket stitch appliqué.

Satin stitch

Sew around the edge of your appliqué motifs using satin stitch (zigzag stitch length 0.5mm and width as required).

Free-motion embroidery

Embroidery is very effective when combined with appliqué. Prepare the motif with fusible webbing or interfacing and tack (baste) if required. Place stabilizer behind the main fabric and proceed as usual, using a hoop if required. Cut away stabilizer from around the appliquéd motif once the stitching is complete.

Satin stitch appliqué: here a 3mm wide zigzag stitch was used.

Free-motion embroidery can be done with general sewing thread, or a specialist decorative thread can be used for contrast.

Hand-sewn appliqué

Hand-sewn appliqué can be used to create decoration and detail on ready-made garments where using a sewing machine would be tricky.

Raw-edge appliqué with invisible stitch

Fabrics that don't fray such as felt can be stitched using invisible stitch without any backing or other treatment. In this sample, felted wool is used to create motifs with holes in.

1 Cut the motifs by freehand or using freezer paper template (see Other Techniques). Use a sharp leather punch to create holes in the felt.

2 Pin and tack (baste) the motifs to the background fabric. Use matching thread and sew around each motif using invisible stitches about 6mm (¼in) apart, but not too close to the edge of the felt. Pull the thread firmly so it sinks into the felt.

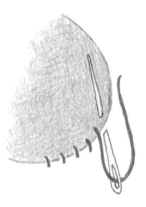

Blanket stitch

Hand-stitched blanket stitch is very effective when worked in contrasting embroidery thread. Blanket stitch can be used with either Raw-Edge Appliqué or Turned Hem Appliqué. This sample is worked on un-backed felt.

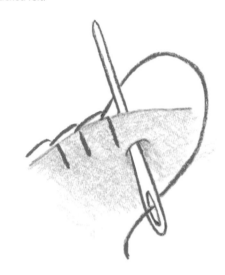

Fine wool felt is ideal for blanket stitch appliqué as the edges do not fray.

Thick recycled wool felt has been cut into pebble shapes then punched with a leather punch to create the Swiss cheese effect.

Turned hem appliqué

Creating neat edges in hand-turned appliqué is tricky. In this technique, freezer paper is used as a temporary template over which the hems are turned before the motif is stitched down by hand.

1 Draw the motif onto the paper side of freezer paper and cut out. Place the waxy side down on the reverse of the appliqué fabric and press with a warm iron to fix the paper to the fabric.

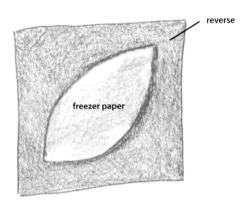
reverse

freezer paper

2 Cut out the motif with a 6mm (¼in) seam allowance.

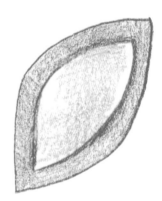

3 Notch inward curves or clip outward curves if required.

4 Turn the seam allowances over to the back and press down, ensuring the fold is right up to the edge of the freezer paper. Press the fabric thoroughly from the front and the back, then remove the freezer paper carefully. Pin from the front with small appliqué pins if required.

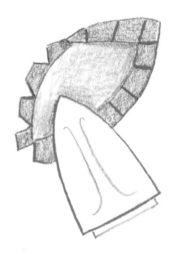

5 Position the motif onto the main fabric, pin and tack (baste) if required, then use invisible stitch to secure all around the motif.

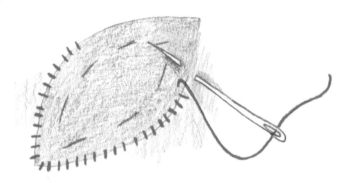

Turned hem appliqué. Fine, striped, silk dupion stands out well against the plain cotton background. Choose a closely matching thread for the most invisible stitches.

Cut and turn appliqué

This is a traditional technique used in Indian embroidery. It works well with lightweight quilting cotton or plain weave fabrics that don't fray too much. The sample shows a zigzag motif but the same technique can be used for many different shapes.

1 Cut a strip of fabric and make a mark along the top edge every 3–6cm (1⅛–2⅜in). Mark in between these marked points 2cm (¾in) down from the top edge. Pin the fabric strip onto the main fabric.

2 Use sharp, fine-pointed scissors to take a small cut from the edge of the fabric strip down to each middle mark.

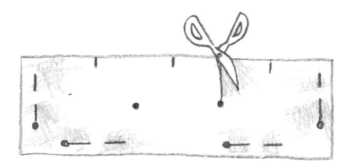

3 Fold the flaps of fabric back, finger press and then use invisible stitch to fasten down the raw edge, using the tip of the needle to turn or fold under the hem as you go. You can trim away more of the folded-under hem fabric if desired.

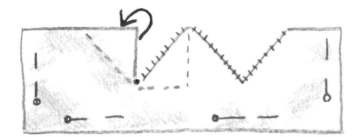

Leather appliqué

Fine leather or suede can be sewn with a fine, sharp, standard sewing needle but a special leather needle is often easier for thicker leather. Fasten the thread on the back of the main fabric, then bring the needle up into the edge of the appliqué. Use invisible stitch or a decorative stitch to attach the appliqué, but do not stitch too close to the edge as leather can tear.

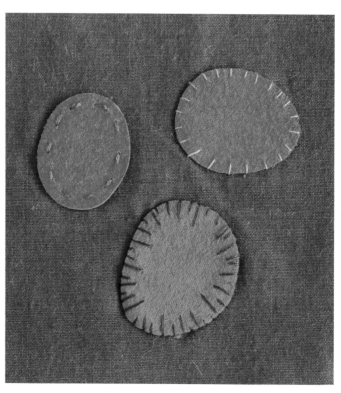

Fine suede pebbles stitched in contrasting threads using a variety of decorative stitches. Blanket stitch could also be used.

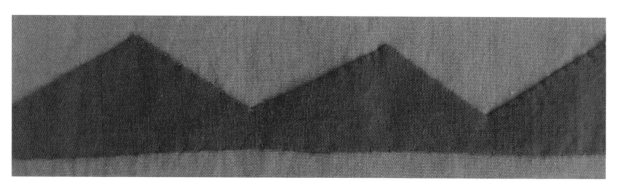

Fine cotton works well for the cut and turn appliqué technique; avoid choosing a fabric that frays readily. Both appliqué and backing fabrics should be similar weights.

3D appliqué

These techniques are for shapes that stand proud of the fabric or that are manipulated into shapes before being applied to the base fabric. These techniques create a dense surface texture using repeating shapes in layers and rows. Each one could easily be developed using variations of shape and application to the base fabric.

MATERIAL AND DESIGN NOTES

- Appliqué motifs that stand proud of the base fabric need to be made in a suitable material which has some body to it. Felt is often ideal as it doesn't fray and it holds its shape well.

- Techniques like these are used in couture fashion where the whole garment is covered in a single technique. Generally this is easier to do before the garment is constructed, but ensure the appliqué matches the grain lines so it hangs correctly.

Circles

Felt circles

This appliqué technique could be used on a number of different shapes. It is based on the principle of making silk petals for fabric flowers, but is highly effective when applied en masse to fabric. Use fine wool felt, boiled wool, Melton or other lightweight non-fraying fabric for the circles. Each felt circle should be made separately before attaching in overlapping rows onto the base fabric; do not be tempted to sew the pleats as you stitch them down onto the fabric as this does not work so well.

1 Cut circles from the chosen fabric about 3cm (1⅛in) in diameter. Take one circle and make a small fold in the edge of it. Use three or four stab stitches to hold the fold and fasten the end securely. Cut the thread and set the petal aside. Continue in this way until all your circle shapes are completed.

Fine wool Melton works perfectly for felt circles; it does not fray and has a nice drape so it sits flat in the finished piece.

2 To apply to the base fabric, start at the bottom of the arrangement and stitch each piece individually by hand, sewing over the folded part and overlapping the shapes as required.

Vertical felt appliqué

Pebble-shapes are applied to the fabric end-on to create a dense texture. Felt is ideal for this technique, but other stiff fabrics could be used, such as organdie, although many more shapes would be required.

1 Cut multiple round (or other shapes) as required according to the density of your chosen fabric.

2 Knot a strong, doubled thread and start on the underside of the base fabric. Bring the needle up through the base fabric, go through the edge of the felt or fabric piece about 6mm (¼in) from the cut edge, then bring the needle back down, almost in the same place. Repeat 2–3 times.

3 Continue to sew the fabric pieces to the base fabric, keeping them close together and alternating colour or shape to create a varied texture.

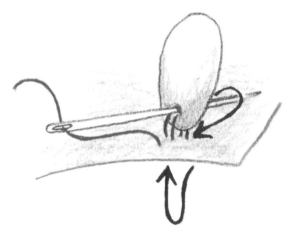

A variety of recycled wool felts have been used to create contrasting colours and textures.

Thick wool felt creates a dense effect.

Petals

This technique requires fine fabrics, which fold and gather up without creating a lot of bulk. Polyester lining fabric or fine habotai silk are ideal. The raw edges will show at the edges of the petals. This technique could be used to make fabric flowers, and the petals can also be attached vertically to the base fabric as in Vertical Felt Appliqué.

1 Cut circles 5cm (2in) in diameter or larger. Fold each circle in half and half again to create quarters.

3 Hand-stitch the petals in rows starting at the top with tips pointing up and the gathered edges pointing down. Overlap each subsequent row so the points cover the gathers and stitches of the previous row. It helps to offset the petals too. Sew four or five strong stitches over the gathers only to hold each petal securely without flattening it.

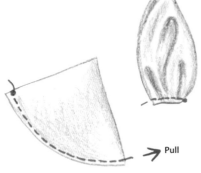

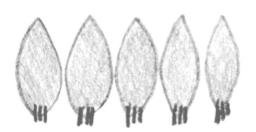

2 Using a knotted thread, sew across the curved raw edge using a small running stitch. Pull up for the gathers and fasten firmly with two or three tiny stitches.

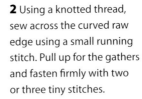

Pull

Small fabric petals stitched together en masse create a dense, decorative texture.

Split circles

This time-consuming but simple technique creates a wave-like effect. The sample shown uses fine linen, and other suitable fabrics include polyester lining, habotai silk, cotton lawn, or any fine soft fabric that will not fray excessively. Experiment with other fabrics to create stiffer, more vertical waves, and thick felt can be used to create bold shapes.

1 Cut circles 6–8cm (2½–3½in) in diameter. Mark a line from edge to centre, along the bias grain of the fabric and cut. Open out the slash and spread the circle.

2 Pin and tack (baste) each circle in position on the base fabric, then hand stitch in place using running stitch.

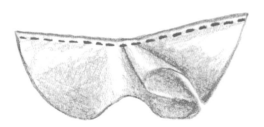

Split circles randomly applied and hand stitched. Alternatively circles can be machine stitched in rows.

Strips

Layers of bias-cut fabric strips create beautiful texture and different fabrics will produce different effects: soft fabrics will flop or lie flat, while stiff organza is ideal for more upright curves. Draw the placement lines on the base fabric first if a very regular design is required.

Raw-edge rows

1 Starting at the top or widest part of the base fabric, pin the first strip in place, then hand or machine stitch.

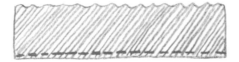

2 Position the next strip so the edges of the strips almost meet, or space them wider apart, ensuring the previous row of stitching is covered. Continue, adding and sewing each strip down by hand or machine before adding the next.

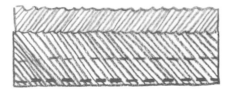

Raw-edge rows using strips 3.5cm (1⅜in) wide; both the front and reverse of the fabric was used to create the alternating stripe effect.

Folded edge.

1 Fold 3–4cm-wide (1–1½in) strips bias-cut fabric in half lengthways, choosing a soft fabric such as silk chiffon or habotai silk. Start at the top of the base fabric and pin the first folded strip in place, with fold towards the top, curving if required. Hand or machine stitch in place.

2 Add the next strip beneath and stitch in place. Continue adding strips increasing the space between strips as you go.

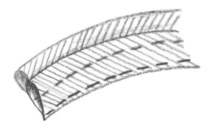

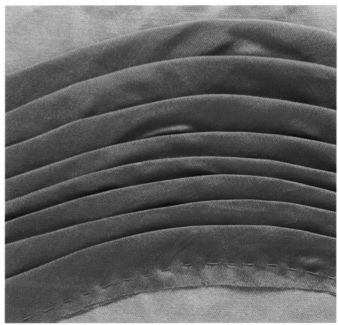

Folded edge: in this sample, the top three rows are spaced 1cm (⅜in) apart, while the lower five rows are spaced 6mm (¼in) apart.

Upright curves

Bias-cut strips will stand upright when stitched in a curve. Stiff fabrics such as silk organza or cotton organdie are very effective for this technique, although softer fabrics such as polyester or silk chiffon can also work.

1 Cut strips 1.5cm (⅝in) wide. Curve and pin the strip into position on the base fabric, stretching slightly, particularly for soft fabrics.

2 Machine stitch along the lower edge of the strip, as illustrated, to curl the top edge. Alternatively, stitch in the centre to curl up both edges.

3 Add the next and each subsequent bias-cut fabric strip so that the edges just overlap.

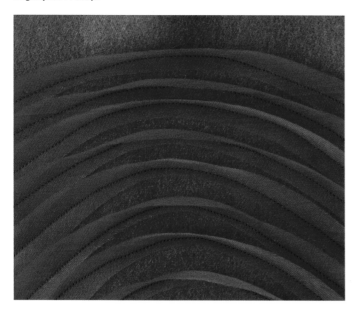

Upright curves in bias-cut silk organza, stitched to sturdy wool fabric.

Looped strips

Thick non-fraying fabrics such as wool felt are best for this technique, or a crisp fabric such as organza or organdie cut on the bias

1 Cut long strips of fabric. Take one strip of fabric and pin the end down on the base fabric; loop the fabric to make a ridge and pin in the furrow where the fabric strip touches the fabric again.

2 Continue to loop the fabric strip, twisting it over as required as you make the ridges, and pinning in the furrows.

3 Hand stitch the strip to the backing in the furrows, using tiny backstitch or running stitch.

Looped strips using bias cut silk organza.

Squares

Cut pieces of fabric are stitched down in lines to create a fluttery, light but dense surface texture. The pieces can be cut in any shape. The sample uses squares cut from bias-cut strips as they will not fray. Lightweight fabrics work well and will all behave differently: try silk chiffon, polyester chiffon, habotai silk or other floaty fabrics.

1 Cut bias strips from your chosen fabric about 4cm (1½in) wide, then cut the strips into squares.

2 Mark horizontal lines across the base fabric 2–4cm (¾–1½in) apart. Pin the squares, point up, overlapping along the line.

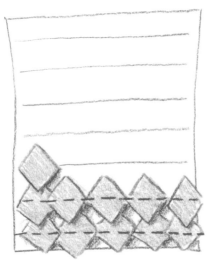

3 Sew across the lines of squares, either through the centre or along the top. Stitching across the centre will keep the shapes quite flat, while stitching the top corners only will allow the squares to float, which is particularly effective on garments.

Squares cut from bias-cut strips.

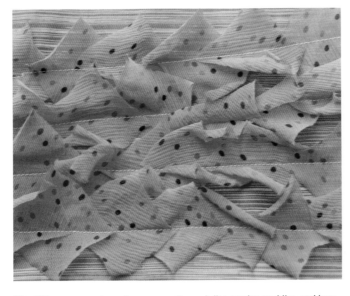

Silk chiffon squares have been sewn through the centre and the curl has been created by steaming the finished piece.

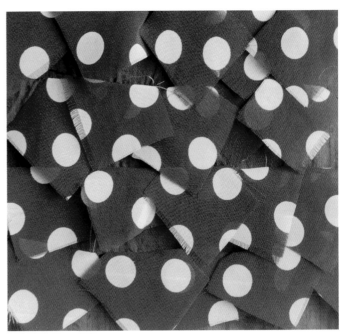

Heavyweight polyester chiffon has been cut into squares (not on the bias) and stitched just across the top points; the sample has then been turned upside down to allow the squares to flop over the stitching.

Loops in rows

Short lengths of ribbon or bias-cut fabric are applied to a base fabric to create loops. The pieces are slightly different lengths and arranged in an irregular design in the two samples shown, but it would also be possible to create a neat, regular design with pieces cut into precise lengths.

Ribbon

1 Use a polyester or silk ribbon of your preferred width, and cut it into short lengths.

2 Starting at the bottom of the design, draw a line across the base fabric. Take a piece of ribbon, fold it in half and position the raw edges on the marked line; pin in place. Place the next ribbon loop slightly above or below the line, butting it right up against the previous ribbon loop. Continue to create an irregular line of folds.

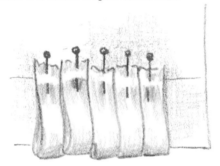

3 Place the piece on the sewing machine with the folded loops facing up and to the left; machine stitch across the raw edges of the ribbon strips.

4 Draw the next guideline 1cm (⅜in) above the first row of stitching and offset the first piece of ribbon so it covers the join between the first two ribbon loops on row 1. Continue as before.

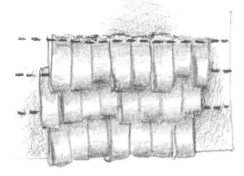

Ribbon loops in rows: here the ribbon is 1.3cm (½in) wide and the lengths are 5–6cm (2½in) long.

Bias-cut fabric

For this to work effectively, your chosen fabric needs to have spring in it, so that when the strips are folded in half, they hold a curve rather than lie flat. Habotai silk was used for this sample. Strips of fabric are cut 3.5cm (1½in) wide and 8–10cm (3–4in) long. As with the Ribbon variation, the strips are applied to the base fabric, offsetting rows. In this sample, the rows are positioned 2cm (¾in) apart.

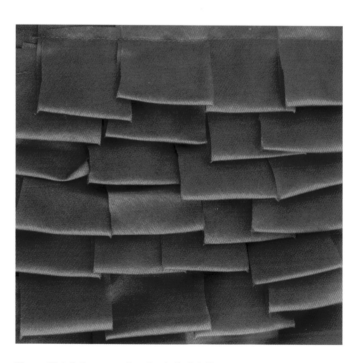

Bias-cut fabric loops made using habotai silk.

Joined felt shapes

In the following techniques, felt fabric shapes are joined together to create an open fabric which can be used alone or applied as a layer, perhaps onto a transparent fabric. Large pieces can become very heavy if hung up bringing the stitching and edges of the felt under strain, so ensure the stitches are firm and that the thread is fastened well. Any shape can be used – geometric tessellating shapes with gaps in between would be very effective.

Butted edge

Cut multiple felt shapes. Working from the reverse side, stitch two felt shapes together, fastening the stitches firmly so that they don't come undone and taking care that the stitches do not show on the front of the fabric. Continue until all the pieces are joined.

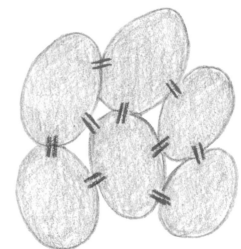

Thick wool felt shapes stitched together with butted edges creates an interesting open fabric which could be layered with other fabrics.

Bar tack joined

Open fabric can be created using longer stitches to attach felt pieces together by making a bar tack with two to three strands of stranded embroidery thread (floss).

1 Working from the reverse side, knot the thread and insert the needle on the edge of a felt shape, so the knot is right on the thin edge of the piece.

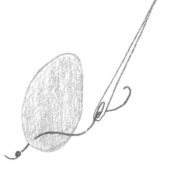

2 Now take a second felt shape and stitch through it, about 6mm (¼in) from the edge, from front to back. Repeat so there are three loose stitches holding the felt shapes together.

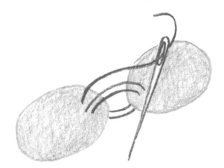

3 Work blanket stitches around all six strands of the joining stitches. Insert the needle under the joining threads from right to left, ensuring the trailing thread is looped under the needle. Pull the stitch tight to complete one stitch.

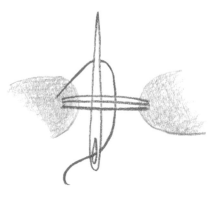

4 Use the needle to slide each stitch along the joining threads so it lies close to the previous one. When you reach the end of the tack, put the needle through to the back of the felt shape and fasten the thread as neatly as possible.

Bar tack joined. Thick wool Melton allows the fastening stitches to be almost invisible. Other fabrics could also be used with contrasting thread.

Reverse appliqué

Reverse appliqué is a traditional technique used to create complex patterns by using plain fabrics and cutting away the surface to reveal one or more layers of fabric underneath. The Mola technique from Panama uses multiple layers of brightly coloured cotton, which are cut away in turn to leave a design of narrow coloured lines. I have included various experimental interpretations of the technique.

MATERIAL AND DESIGN NOTES

- For the top layers of fabric choose ones that do not fray too much – the bottom layer can be anything as it will not be cut. Cotton lawn is an ideal fabric.

- Fine-pointed embroidery scissors are essential to get close to the stitching and create neat cuts.

- The design is marked on the top fabric so use a vanishing pen as raw-edge reverse appliqué is not easily washed.

Basic method

1 Layer two or more fabrics together right side up. Transfer or draw the design onto the top fabric layer. Machine stitch the outline of the design, or hand stitch with backstitch, running stitch or a decorative stitch.

Raw-edge reverse appliqué.

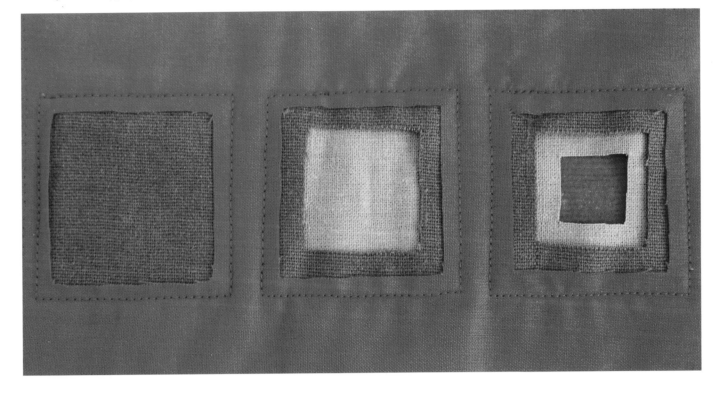

2 Pinch and separate the fabric layers within the stitched area, making sure you have hold of the top layer only. Using small, sharp, fine-pointed scissors, cut a small snip in the top layer.

3 Cut away the top layer of fabric within the stitched area up to 6mm (¼in) from the stitched edge, or closer if it will not fray.

4 Draw a second design on the next fabric layer; sew around the design as in step 1. Cut away as in steps 2 and 3. Continue in this way for the number of fabric layers being worked to achieve the effect you desire.

5 The edges of the reverse appliqué can be left raw, or if you prefer, you can turn the raw edges under and hand stitch in place (see Needle-Turned Reverse Appliqué).

Reverse appliqué variations

Reverse appliqué, machine stitched felt
Felt, or fine leather, can be stitched and cut away close to the stitching without risk of fraying. The stitching can be worked by hand or machine. No stabilizer is required when working with felt, making it particularly suitable for large pieces stitched by machine.

Shadow work, hand-stitched

Shadow work is essentially the same technique as raw-edge reverse appliqué (see Basic Method), but using transparent fabrics to create a shadow effect. Two layers of fabric are stitched together with one layer cut away to reveal the design. Silk organza is ideal for this technique as it is stiff and doesn't fray too much, and the finer the silk the better. Stitch the design with matching thread, as fine as possible for almost-invisible stitching. You can even use long threads unravelled from the edge of the fabric itself.

1 Layer two pieces of silk organza and tack (baste) around the edges. Trace the design onto the top fabric layer using vanishing pen.

2 Start the stitching by making two tiny backstitches (do not use a knot), and work tiny running stitches around the drawn line. An appliqué needle will help you to make the stitches as small as possible. To finish, fasten the thread with backstitch.

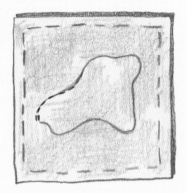

3 Separate the layers ready to cut away the top layer (see Basic Method, step 2).

4 Trim the top layer to within 2–3mm (⅛in) of the sewn edge (depending on how much the organza frays).

Shadow work, machined

This is the same as hand-stitched shadow work but the design is machine-stitched. Machine stitching small curves can be tricky. Work slowly and with a short stitch length. Alternatively, use free-motion machine embroidery.

1 Tack (baste) together the two layers of fabric and draw out the design (see Shadow Work, Hand-Stitched, step 1).

2 Use small machine stitches to follow the design, reducing the stitch length to 0.5mm at the start and end to finish the stitching invisibly. Pull the threads to the back and knot if required.

3 Cut away the top layer following steps 3 and 4 of Shadow Work, Hand-Stitched.

Machine-stitched shadow work in straight stitch. Satin stitch or other dense embroidery stitches could also be used.

Hand-stitched shadow work – the organza used in this sample is quite coarse, but the white silk Scalloped Cape uses a much finer organza, which allows for a more detailed design.

Project Idea:
Scalloped Cape

Use a basic evening cape pattern and add
scalloped edges all around.

Techniques: Scalloped Edge and Shadow Work
Material: Fine quality silk organza

• Add scalloped edges to a cape pattern (see Holes, Cut Outs
  and Negative Shapes: Scalloped Edges)

• Cut two layers of the cape pattern and sew together, leaving
  a small gap on the back neck for turning. Trim the seam
  allowances to 5mm (¼in). Turn neatly and press flat. Sew up
  the opening.

• Trace the required design, using vanishing marker pen. Work
  the design using threads pulled from the leftover fabric so
  the stitches are invisible. Cut the shadow work details from
  the inside layer of the cape working on the reverse side (see
  the detail photograph).

Satin stitch reverse appliqué

Where the top fabric might fray a lot, machined satin stitch can stabilize the edge and create a neat, decorative finish. This technique can be applied to a variety of materials but is particularly suitable for lightweight fabrics. Tear-away stabilizer is used underneath the fabrics to prevent the fine fabrics from getting snarled up in the machine's needle plate or from puckering as you stitch. You should leave the stabilizer in place until you have cut away the top layer of fabric as this makes it easier to manipulate.

1 Cut the top and base fabrics and the stabilizer to the same size. Transfer the design to the top fabric layer *before* you put the fabric sandwich together. Tack (baste) the fabric sandwich together making sure the stabilizer is at the bottom.

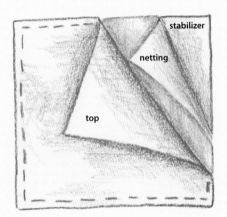

2 Set the satin stitch using 0.5mm stitch length and 2mm stitch width, or as wide as required for the design. Start on a corner or straight edge and slowly sew along the lines of the design. Pivot at corners or tight curves with the needle down on the right- hand side of the satin stitching. (It is a good idea to practise first before starting on the finished piece, to get the hang of curves and corners.)

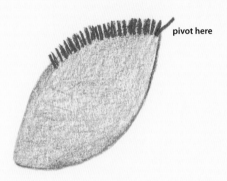

3 When the stitching is complete, pull the threads through to the back, knot and cut. Separate the layers ready to cut away the top layer (see Basic Method, step 2). Cut away the top fabric cutting very close to the edge of the satin stitching, but making sure you don't cut the satin stitched threads at all. If top fabric threads remain in the edge of the satin stitching, first remove the stabilizer, then fold the base fabric back out of the way so the remaining threads stick up, and trim using fine-pointed scissors.

Fold netting back

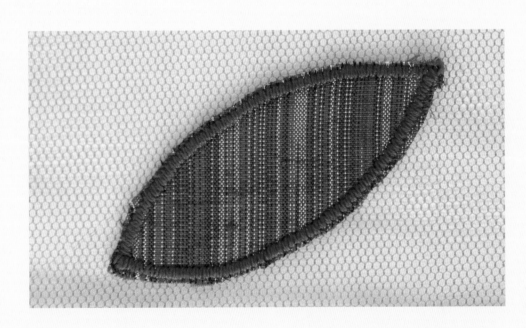

Satin stitch reverse appliqué. The contrast of the silk and the fine net creates a dramatic effect.

Needle-turned reverse appliqué

In this version of reverse appliqué, the layers are slashed and the top fabric folded back. It is also known as folded reverse appliqué. It works particularly well where the fabrics used are fine and turn under easily. Cotton lawn is ideal.

1 Transfer the design onto the top fabric. Layer two or three fabrics. Outline the marked design by hand or machine stitching.

2 Mark the line of the slashing and separate the fabrics. Make a very tiny snip in the top fabric right on the marked line. Carefully cut along the marked line, leaving a few millimetres at each end to allow the fabric to turn.

3 Fold the fabric under, utilizing the tip of a needle to tuck it under where the underlap is narrow. Use tiny, fine, appliqué pins to hold in place and tack (baste) if required. Knot a single thread and bring it up from the underside, coming out just on the edge of the fold. Use tiny, invisible stitches to hold the folded edge in place.

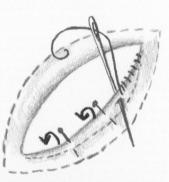

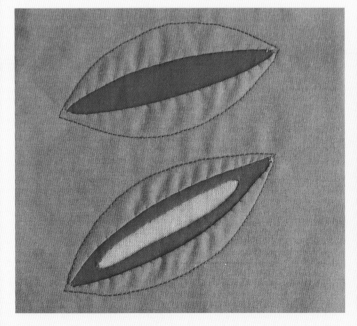

Needle-turned reverse appliqué. To create the three-colour version, mark and cut the middle layer of fabric to reveal the base fabric and continue as before.

Slashed boiled wool

This technique creates an openwork wool fabric which can be used alone or as an applied layer. Use hand-wash only wool, which is suitable for felting, such as an old jumper or wool jersey fabric. (If using a jumper, cut it into flat pieces by cutting along the side seams, around the armholes and across the shoulders.) The slashes made in the wool are sealed when it felts, so the edges do not fray. All wool fabrics will shrink differently so start with a piece much larger than you need and cut it down to the right size.

1 Place the wool fabric on a cutting mat. Using a rotary cutter or large pair of scissors, cut slashes in the wool. You can use a metal ruler with the rotary cutter, but take care that the blade can't slip onto your hand.

2 To felt it, wash the slashed wool fabric in your washing machine on a 60°C cycle.

3 Hang the felted fabric up to dry, then iron on medium heat with lots of steam to get all the creases out. Horizontal slashes will curl outwards – you can press them flat or leave then to curl. Vertical slashes usually do not curl so much.

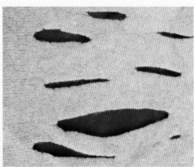

Different effects are achieved by slashing horizontally across the knitted grain or vertically along the lines of the rib in the knit. The size of the slashes and the distance between them will also affect the final effect created after felting. The red fabric has small slashes vertically along the knitted rib, while in the pink sample, the slashes are longer and run across the grain horizontally.

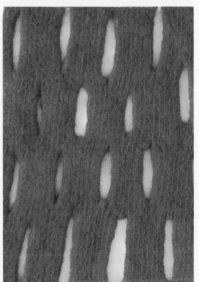

Holes, cut outs and negative shapes

Holes and decorative edging can be used to frame a fabric underneath or simply to create a neat edging. Cut-out holes can be used as windows to reveal layers beneath while scalloped edges can be overlapped to create a dense surface texture. A hole of any shape can be made, as long as it is stitched, clipped, turned and pressed carefully. Scallops likewise can be made in any shape, as the Seaweed Edge Scarf shows.

MATERIAL AND DESIGN NOTES

- In the samples shown, the lining fabric is the same as the main fabric so it barely shows on the opening edge once it has been turned. A contrasting fabric would show as a line around the edge of the opening.
- Medium-weight fabrics such as quilting cotton work well. Thick fabrics will not lie flat when turned as the seam is bulky. Back fabrics with a matching, light fabric, such as silk organza (if the reverse will not be seen) so you can have a neat opening without the bulk.
- The seam allowances will show through on transparent or light fabrics, or if the backing is darker than the front fabric.

Basic method

Note: This describes the making of a square or rectangular hole.

1 Mark the shape of the opening on the reverse of the lining fabric. Place the main fabric and lining fabrics right sides together.

2 Machine stitch around the lines of the marked shape, using a short stitch length and starting in the middle of one of the long sides. Do not reverse to start and end the thread, but pull the threads to the back and knot.

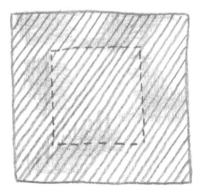

3 Cut through both layers of fabric inside the square in an X-shape, right up to the stitching but not through it. Cut away the triangles of fabric to within 3mm (⅛in) of the stitching.

4 Turn the lining through the hole to the back. Carefully manipulate the edges of the fabric so that the hole is neat. Press the hole thoroughly so that there are no wrinkles or puckers.

5 Place the contrast fabric behind the fabric with the hole in it, lining the pieces up carefully with plenty of overlap behind the opening. Pin and tack (baste) if required.

6 Sew through all layers to join the pieces together. Keep the stitching an even distance from the edge of the hole, either by using a guide foot or by keeping the edge of the machine foot on the edge of the hole, and pivot at the corners.

Square or rectangular hole.

Circular hole

This is created in the same way as the square in the Basic Method, but by stitching in a circle. Cut away the fabric within the circle up to 3mm (⅛in) from the stitching. If the fabric is too thick to allow it to turn neatly, cut notches in the seam allowance. Turn and press, then add backing fabric as required.

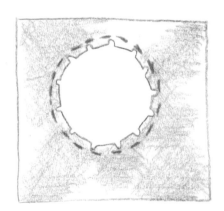

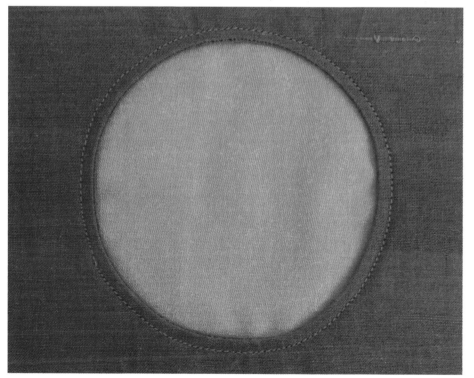

Circular hole.

Project Idea:
Seaweed Edge Scarf

This scarf is created using an irregular scallop edge design based on seaweed.

Technique: Scalloped Edge
Material: Light cotton or lawn

- First create a template using seaweed as your inspiration. The template does not have to be the whole design; you can draw around the same small template several times, moving it slightly, turning it over and adapting it to get an irregular edge.

- Take a piece of fabric measuring 1 x 2m (1⅛ x 2¼yd). Fold in half lengthways with right sides together, and pin the raw edges. Use the template to draw the scallop edging design along both ends, from side to side.

- Starting from the folded edge at one end of the scarf, stitch the drawn line carefully, using tiny stitches. (Alternatively, draw a guideline on the fabric and use free-motion stitching, ensuring the stitches are small.)

- At the raw edge side, sew up the long side of the scarf using a 1.5cm (⅝in) seam allowance, and leaving a 15cm (6in) gap unsewn half way along. Sew the seaweed scallops at the other end, finishing at the folded edge.

- Cut away the excess fabric from the seaweed scallops leaving a 5mm (¼in) seam allowance. Clip and notch as required. Turn the right way out through the gap left in the side seam. Push out all the scallops with a knitting needle. Press flat and hand sew the opening closed.

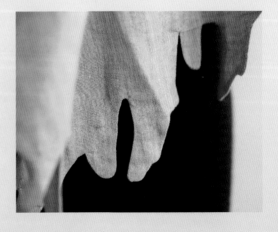

Scalloped Edge

The scalloped edge can be used for shaped hems on garments or in layers to create textured effects. For a perfectly neat finish, accurate machine stitching is required, as well as a template. To create a template, use adhesive-tape rolls or circle templates to draw out the curves onto card and cut out. Measure accurately and ensure there is a large enough gap between the scallops for them to turn out properly: 5–6mm (¼in) is best for a light fabric while thicker fabrics will require a wider gap.

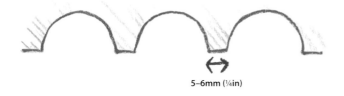

5–6mm (¼in)

Selecting fabrics

Very thick fabrics are hard to turn out neatly and would need to be extra-large scallops. Lightweight fabrics are fine but be aware that the seam allowances will show through. Medium-weight fabrics are ideal. If the reverse side does not show, you could use matching silk organza as the lining fabric, as this will allow a thicker fabric to be used without creating bulky seams, but it will need to be the same colour as the edge will show.

Basic method

1 Draw around the template on the reverse side of one of the fabrics, close to the edge.

2 Place the two pieces of fabric right sides together, with the marked line facing up. Pin in place, including through the scallops, and tack (baste) if required.

3 Machine stitch along the marked line using a 2mm stitch length. Go very slowly to make sure the curves are accurate. Pivot the needle to make the corners and to adjust to the curves.

4 Cut out the scallops about 6mm (¼in) from the stitching, and cut a slit into the narrow gaps between scallops. Notch the curved edges, but not too close to the stitching.

5 Turn the right way out and use a knitting needle to push the corners and edges out. Finger press, manipulating the fabric so that the lining does not show on the front side. Press thoroughly.

Fine cotton creates neat scallops.

Scallop variations

These are all created using the Basic Method, clipping and notching the curves (see Other Techniques).

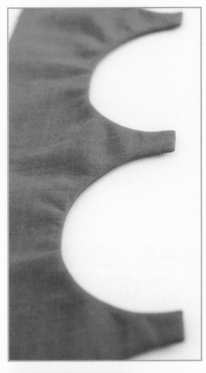

Inverted scallops – this template has 1cm (⅜in) gaps between the circles.

Bunting – this template has 1cm (⅜in) gaps between the flag-shapes.

Squares – this template has 2cm (¾in) gaps between the squares.

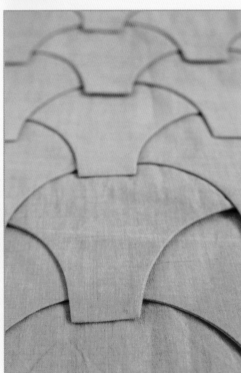

Overlapping inverted scallops: several rows of inverted scallops have been overlapped in alternating layers; each layer is stitched to the backing fabric before the next is added.

In-seam trims

Decorative trimmings can be added between two layers of fabric and sewn together when making a seam to create an interesting effect on the front. They can be used in garments or in patchwork or pieced fabrics. The fabric can be folded back so the trim protrudes along an edge, or be pressed flat with the insertion standing proud of the fabric as shown in the Basic Method.

MATERIAL AND DESIGN NOTES

- You could even try using broken zips, bias-cut strips or any kind of decorative edging in the seam.

- Half-zips should be tacked along the seam line, with teeth to the left. Sew with a zip foot.

- Fringe and bobbles should be sewn with the decorative edge pointing inwards on the main fabric so the braid part is contained in the seam allowance.

3 Hand tack (baste) the trim in place along the centre, so you are sewing right on the seam line.

4 Place the other piece of fabric on top with right sides facing, making sure the raw edges are matched; pin in place.

5 Sew the seam with the tacking (basting) facing up. Follow the line of the tacking (basting) very precisely. Remove the tacking (basting), turn out and press flat, or open the piece out and press the seam so the trim stands proud.

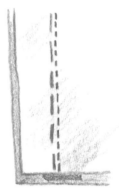

Basic method

1 Mark the seam line accurately (this is usually 1.5cm/⅝in) with tailor's chalk or marking pen on the right side of one piece of fabric.

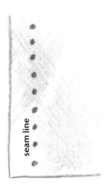

seam line

2 Pin the trim along the marked seam line. If there is a particular edge that you want to have showing, make sure that edge is the one facing inwards, with the edge to be hidden facing the raw edge. Make sure the centre of the trim is positioned on the seam line.

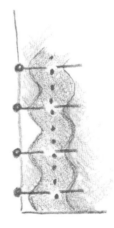

The basic method is described and shown using ricrac.

In-seam trim variations

Felt shapes

Cut shapes from felt, either in a long strip with one straight edge, or as individual pieces. If using a long strip follow the Basic Method. If using individual shapes, cut each felt piece with a long extension and straight edge (see diagram). Line up the pieces with the straight edges on the raw edge of the fabric and the shapes pointing to the left. Butt the pieces up to each other if required.

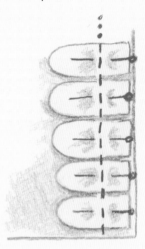

Place the other piece of fabric on top and pin through all the layers. Continue as for the Basic Method.

Piping

Piping cord or double-knitting weight yarn is encased in a matching or co-ordinating fabric.

1 Measure the thickness of the piping cord or double-knitting weight yarn then add 3cm (1⅛in) to work out the total width of the fabric strip required.

2 Wrap the fabric around the cord/yarn, right side out, and tack (baste) by hand. Using a zip foot, machine stitch close to the cord/yarn.

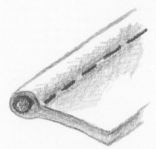

3 Position the finished piping on the seam line with the stitching on the marked line.

4 Pin and tack (baste) all layers. Stitch from the tacked (basted) side, following the line of stitches. Use a zip foot to get as close as possible to the piping.

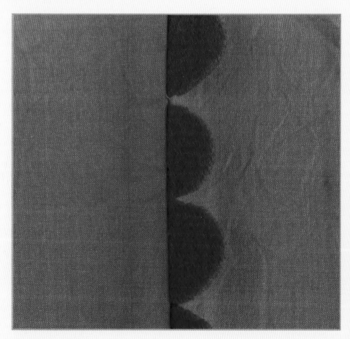

Wool felt could be cut into any shapes and inserted into the seam.

Piping: double-knitting weight yarn was used here rather than piping cord.

Project Idea:
Ricrac Apron

This apron is made using a pieced, patchwork pattern available from www.ruthsinger.com. The side panels are made of five sections with the braid applied between them rather than on the surface.

Technique: In-Seam Trim
Material: Fine black linen and white ricrac

• Cut sections of patchwork. Apply the ricrac braid on the seam line, centring it carefully so exactly half shows when the seam is sewn (see In-Seam Trims: Basic Method).

• Sew each section and press the seam allowance open on the back; then, from the front, press the braid so it lies downwards towards the hem of the garment, or press it both up and down so it stands upright away from the fabric.

• Make up the garment following the pattern instructions.

SUPPLIERS

UK

Broadwick Silks
www.broadwicksilks.com
Specialist silk supplier for silk dupion, taffeta and organza.

Cloth House
47 & 98 Berwick Street, London, W1
www.clothhouse.com
The finest fabric shops in the UK. Also sells vintage ribbon.

VV Rouleaux
www.vvrouleaux.com
102 Marylebone Lane, London, W1
Luxury ribbon and trimming specialists.

Kleins
www.kleins.co.uk
5 Noel Street, London, W1F 8GB
Professional haberdashery and tools.

MacCulloch and Wallis
www.macculloch-wallis.co.uk
25–26 Dering Street, London, W1S 1AT
Specialist fabrics, tailoring and haberdashery supplies including interfacing.

Cheap Fabrics
www.cheapfabrics.co.uk
Good source of silk dupion and other fabrics.

Rag Rescue
www.ragrescue.co.uk
Vintage fabrics and trimmings.

Wingham Wool Work
www.winghamwoolwork.co.uk
Yarn, wool tops and wool stuffing.

The Eternal Maker
www.eternalmaker.com
Wide selection of fabrics including cotton gingham, 32mm silk ribbon and metric (centimetre) grid interfacing.

Cotton Patch
www.cottonpatch.co.uk
Quilting supplies including extensive range of tools, quilt wadding and freezer paper.

Organic Cotton
www.organiccotton.biz
Fair-trade organic cottons in a wide range of colours

Ray Stitch
www.raystitch.co.uk
99 Essex Road, London, N1 2SJ
Wide range of contemporary fabrics including organic cotton and fine haberdashery plus wool felt.

Fair Trade Fabrics
www.fairtradefabric.co.uk
Organic cotton.

Oakshott Fabrics
www.oakshottfabrics.com
Fine quilting cotton.

Crafty Ribbons
www.craftyribbons.com
Narrow silk ribbon.

House of Smocking
www.smocking.co.uk
English Smocking resources including transfers and pleaters.

Jaycotts
www.jaycotts.co.uk
Sewing machine accessories and haberdashery.

Textile Society
www.textilesociety.org.uk
Annual Antique Textiles fair in Manchester and London.

Stitch Craft Create
www.stitchcraftcreate.co.uk
Fabrics and haberdashery.

Online resources are listed on www.ruthsinger.com

US

www.purlsoho.com
Good for printed and plain cottons and other fabrics, as well as wool felt.

www.rickrack.com
Vintage fabrics.

www.nearseanaturals.com
Organic and sustainable fabrics.

www.moodfabrics.com
Fashion and dressmaking fabrics.

www.britexfabrics.com
Fashion fabrics and silks.

Japan

www.fabrictales.com
Japanese fabrics.

Canada

www.valdani.com
Embroidery threads.

Australia

www.kelanifabric.com.au
Quilting and patterned fabrics.

www.tessuti-shop.com
Fashion fabrics.

www.easternsilk.com.au
Silk fabrics.

www.beautifulsilks.com
Silk fabrics.

Germany

www.volksfaden.de
Craft and patchwork fabrics.

SUGGESTED READING

Conlon, J., *Fine Embellishment Techniques: Classic Details for Today's Clothing.* Taunton Press, 2001

Gardner, S. , *A-Z of Smocking: A Complete Manual for the Beginner Through to the Advanced Smocker.* Country Bumpkin Publications, 2000.

Guerrier, K., *The Encyclopedia of Quilting and Patchwork Techniques.* Search Press, 2001.

Hart, A. and North, S., *Historical Fashion in Detail: The 17th and 18th Centuries.* V&A Publications 2000.

Johnston, L., *Nineteenth Century Fashion in Detail.* V&A Publications 2005.

Lewis, A., *Ribbons and Trims: Embellishing Furniture, Furnishings and Home Accessories.* Jacqui Small 2007.

Marsh, G., *Eighteenth Century Embroidery Techniques.* Guild of Master Craftsmen Publications 2006.

Mendes, V. and Wilcox, C., *Modern Fashion in Detail.* V&A Publications 1991.

Pitman, K. (ed)., *Every Kind of Smocking.* Search Press 1985.

Rayment, J., *Creative Tucks and Textiles for Quilts and Embroidery.* Batsford 2004.

Reid, A., *Stitch Magic: Sculpting Fabric with Stitch.* A&C Black 2011.

Rutzky, J. and Palmer, C. K., *Shadowfolds: Surprisingly Easy-to-make Geometric Designs in Fabric.* Kodansha 2011.

Shaeffer, C., *Sew Any Fabric: A Quick Reference Guide to Fabrics from A to Z.* KP Books, 2004.

Singer, R., *Sew it Up: A Modern Manual of Practical and Decorative Sewing Techniques.* Kyle Books, 2008. (*Note:* This title published in the US as The Sewing Bible by Potter Craft.)

Singer, R., *Sew Eco: Sewing Sustainable and Re-used Fabrics.* A&C Black, 2010.

Tellier-Loumange, F., *The Art of Embroidery: Inspirational Stitches, Textures and Surfaces.* Thames & Hudson 2006.

Willoughby, A., *49½ Skirts.* A&C Black, 2008.

Wolff, C., *The Art of Manipulating Fabric.* Krause Publications, 1996.

ABOUT THE AUTHOR

Unlike many textile artists, Ruth came to a creative career relatively late. She learned woodwork as a small child, rather than sewing, although the love of textiles started early too. She started dressmaking at the age of 12 and spent her teens making things from fabric, but ultimately chose an academic career path and read Medieval Studies at university, followed by a Masters in Museum Studies. Ruth's love of textiles continued through this period and she became fascinated by medieval textile techniques, particularly clothing construction and braiding. Her aim was to become a curator of costume and indulge her love of textiles professionally. Despite a few brief forays into cataloguing costume, she eventually found a new love of communication and sharing, and focussed on museum education work for several years. Finally, she got a job in her favourite place, the Victoria and Albert Museum in London. She spent three years there, absorbing huge amounts of inspiration and meeting artists and craftspeople, until the jealousy became too much, and she left her job to make, teach and write about textiles.

Since 2005 she has exhibited extensively in the UK and overseas, and won several commissions and awards. She was Maker in Residence at Bilston Craft Gallery in 2007, and later was commissioned by Derby Museums to create new work inspired by their African collections. In 2012 she completed a major commission from Shire Hall Gallery, Stafford, inspired by photographs of Victorian women criminals from when the building was a courtroom. She has also won the Craftspace Prize for her collection Monumental Folly in 2012.

Ruth's work continues to be heavily inspired by historic textiles, museum objects, personal heritage, memory and stories. She uses natural and sustainable textiles combined with fabric manipulation and other creative techniques, often developed from her own study of historical textiles. Her work has featured in *The Guardian, the Daily Mail, Elle Decoration* and in a number of books, and she has authored two previous books (see Suggested Reading).

Ruth works extensively in education, with schools, adults and community groups, and she particularly enjoys collaborating with museums and in developing innovative community-led projects. She runs regular fabric manipulation workshops, sewing classes, creative events, parties, talks and much more at the Ruth Singer Studio in Leicester city centre.

For more details visit www.ruthsinger.com

ACKNOWLEDGEMENTS

It is impossible to work back to where a book like this began, but it has been in my mind for at least five years. I am delighted that F&W Media have supported me in taking it from inspiration to printed page, and I would like to thank all of them for helping to create this book. I also owe great thanks to my agent Sallyanne Sweeney of Watson Little Ltd for her support. My family are also vital to my creativity and are a huge support to me practically and I owe them endless thanks for everything they do. This book, and indeed my whole career and creative life would not exist if it were not for museums like the V&A (where I was so lucky to work for three years) who preserve and exhibit the extraordinary textiles of the past and present. I dedicate this book to the millions of anonymous stitchers of the world who would be astonished to find their work in museums hundreds of years after they have gone, inspiring another generation. I hope that I can do the same.

INDEX

A DAVID & CHARLES BOOK

© F&W Media International, Ltd 2013

David & Charles is an imprint of F&W Media International, Ltd
Brunel House, Forde Close, Newton Abbot, TQ12 4PU, UK

F&W Media International, Ltd is a subsidiary of F+W Media, Inc
10151 Carver Road, Suite #200, Blue Ash, OH 45242, USA

ISBN-13: 978-1-4463-0246-0 hardback
ISBN-10: 1-4463-0246-6 hardback

ISBN-13: 978-1-4463-0247-7 paperback
ISBN-10: 1-4463-0247-4 paperback

Printed in China by RR Donnelley for
F&W Media International, Ltd
Brunel House, Forde Close, Newton Abbot, TQ12 4PU, UK

10 9 8 7 6 5 4 3 2 1

Acquisitions Editor: Sarah Callard
Editor: Jeni Hennah
Project Editor: Cheryl Brown
Art Editor: Jodie Lystor
Photographers: Lorna Yabsley and Jack Kirby
Illustrator: Gina Barrett
Senior Production Controller: Kelly Smith

F+W Media publishes high quality books on a wide range of subjects.
For more great book ideas visit: **www.stitchcraftcreate.co.uk**